Alexandria and her Schools

Charles Kingsley

Contents

ALEXANDRIA AND HER SCHOOLS

BY

Charles Kingsley

ALEXANDRIA AND HER SCHOOLS {1}

PREFACE

I should not have presumed to choose for any lectures of mine such a subject as that which I have tried to treat in this book. The subject was chosen by the Institution where the lectures were delivered. Still less should I have presumed to print them of my own accord, knowing how fragmentary and crude they are. They were printed at the special request of my audience. Least of all, perhaps, ought I to have presumed to publish them, as I have done, at Cambridge, where any inaccuracy or sciolism (and that such defects exist in these pages, I cannot but fear) would be instantly detected, and severely censured: but nevertheless, it seemed to me that Cambridge was the fittest place in which they could see the light, because to Cambridge I mainly owe what little right method or sound thought may be found in them, or indeed, in anything which I have ever written. In the heyday of youthful greediness and ambition, when the mind, dazzled by the vastness and variety of the universe, must needs know everything, or rather know about everything, at once and on the spot, too many are apt, as I have been in past years, to complain of Cambridge studies as too dry and narrow: but as time teaches the student, year by year, what is really required for an understanding of the objects with which he meets, he begins to find that his University, in as far as he has really received her teaching into himself, has given him, in her criticism, her mathematics, above all, in Plato, something which all the popular knowledge, the lectures and institutions of the day, and even good books themselves, cannot give, a boon more precious than learning; namely, the art of learning. That instead of casting into his lazy lap treasures which he would not have known how to use, she has taught him to mine for them himself; and has by her wise refusal to gratify his intellectual greediness, excited his hunger, only that he may be the stronger to hunt and till for his own subsistence; and thus, the deeper he drinks, in after years, at fountains wisely forbidden to him while he was a Cambridge student, and sees his old companions growing up into sound-headed and sound-hearted practical men, liberal and expansive, and yet with a firm standing- ground for thought and action, he learns to complain less and less of Cambridge studies, and more and more of that conceit and haste of his own, which kept him from reaping the full advantage of her training.

These Lectures, as I have said, are altogether crude and fragmentary-- how, indeed, could they be otherwise, dealing with so vast a subject, and so long a period of time? They are meant neither as Essays nor as Orations, but simply as a collection of hints to those who may wish to work out the subject for themselves; and, I trust, as giving some glimpses of a central idea, in the light of which the spiritual history of Alexandria, and perhaps of other countries also, may be seen to have in itself a coherence and organic method.

I was of course compelled, by the circumstances under which these Lectures were delivered, to keep clear of all points which are commonly called "controversial." I cannot but feel that this was a gain, rather than a loss; because it forced me, if I wished to give any interpretation at all of Alexandrian thought, any Theodicy at all of her fate, to refer to laws which I cannot but believe to be deeper, wider, more truly eternal than the points which cause most of our modern controversies, either theological or political; laws which will, I cannot but believe also, reassert themselves, and have to be reasserted by all wise teachers, very soon indeed, and it may be under most novel embodiments, but without any change in their eternal spirit.

For I may say, I hope, now (what if said ten years ago would have only excited laughter), that I cannot but subscribe to the opinion of the many wise men who believe that Europe, and England as an integral part thereof, is on the eve of a revolution, spiritual and political, as vast and awful as that which took place at the Reformation; and that, beneficial as that revolution will doubtless be to the destinies of mankind in general, it depends upon the wisdom and courage of each nation individually, whether that great deluge shall issue, as the Reformation did, in a fresh outgrowth of European nobleness and strength or usher in, after pitiable confusions and sorrows, a second Byzantine age of stereotyped effeminacy and imbecility. For I have as little sympathy with those who prate so loudly of the progress of the species, and the advent of I know-not-what Cockaigne of universal peace and plenty, as I have with those who believe on the strength of "unfulfilled prophecy," the downfall of Christianity, and the end of the human race to be at hand. Nevertheless, one may well believe that prophecy will be fulfilled in this great crisis, as it is in every great crisis, although one be unable to conceive by what method of symbolism the drying up of the Euphrates can be twisted to signify the fall of Constantinople: and one can well believe that a day of judgment is at hand, in which for every nation and institution, the wheat will be sifted out and gathered into God's garner, for the use of future generations, and the chaff burnt up with that fire unquenchable which will try every man's work, without being of opinion that after a few more years are over, the great majority of the human race will be consigned hopelessly to never-ending torments.

If prophecy be indeed a divine message to man; if it be anything but a cabbala, useless either to the simple-minded or to the logical, intended only for the plaything of a few devout fancies, it must declare the unchangeable laws by which the unchangeable God is governing, and has always governed, the human race; and therefore only by understanding what has happened, can we understand what will happen; only by understanding history, can we understand prophecy; and that not merely by picking out--too often arbitrarily and unfairly--a few names and dates from the records of all the ages, but by trying to discover its organic laws, and the causes which produce in nations, creeds, and systems, health and disease, growth, change, decay and death. If, in one small corner of this vast field, I shall have thrown a single ray of light upon these subjects--if I shall have done anything in these pages towards illustrating the pathology of a single people, I shall believe that I have done better service to the Catholic Faith and the Scriptures, than if I did really "know the times and the seasons, which the Father has kept in His own hand." For by the former act I may have helped to make some one man more prudent and brave to see and to do what God requires of him; by the latter I could only add to that paralysis of superstitious fear, which is already but too common among us, and but too likely to hinder us from doing our duty manfully against our real foes, whether it be pestilence at home or tyranny abroad.

These last words lead me to another subject, on which I am bound to say a few words. I have, at the end of these Lectures, made some allusion to the present war. To have entered further into political questions would have been improper in the place where those Lectures were delivered: but I cannot refrain from saying here something more on this matter; and that, first, because all political questions have their real root in moral and spiritual ones, and not (as too many fancy) in questions merely relating to the balance of power or commercial economy, and are (the world being under the guidance of a spiritual, and not a physical Being) finally decided on those spiritual grounds, and according to the just laws of the kingdom of God; and, therefore, the future political horoscope of the East depends entirely on the present spiritual state of its inhabitants, and of us who have (and rightly) taken up their cause; in short, on many of those questions on which I have touched in these Lectures: and next, because I feel bound, in justice to myself, to guard against any mistake about my meaning or supposition that I consider the Turkish empire a righteous thing, or one likely to stand much longer on the face of God's earth.

The Turkish empire, as it now exists, seems to me an altogether unrighteous and worthless thing. It stands no longer upon the assertion of the great truth of Islam, but on the merest brute force and oppression. It has long since lost the only excuse which one race can have for holding another in subjection; that which we have for taking on ourselves the tutelage of the Hindoos, and which Rome had for its tutelage of the Syrians and Egyptians; namely, the governing with tolerable justice those who cannot govern themselves, and making them better and more prosperous people, by compelling them to submit to law. I do not know when this excuse is a sufficient one. God showed that it was so for several centuries in the case of the Romans; God will show whether it is in the case of our Indian empire: but this I say, that the Turkish empire has not even that excuse to plead; as is proved by the patent fact that the whole East, the very garden of the old world, has become a desert and a ruin under the upas-blight of their government.

As for the regeneration of Turkey, it is a question whether the regeneration of any nation which has sunk, not into mere valiant savagery, but into effete and profligate luxury, is possible. Still more is it a question whether a regeneration can be effected, not by the rise of a new spiritual idea (as in the case of the Koreish), but simply by more perfect material appliances, and commercial prudence. History gives no instance, it seems to me, of either case; and if our attempt to regenerate Greece by freeing it has been an utter failure, much more, it seems to me, would any such attempt fail in the case of the Turkish race. For what can be done with a people which has lost the one great quality which was the tenure of its existence, its military skill? Let any one read the accounts of the Turkish armies in the fifteenth, sixteenth, and seventeenth centuries, when they were the tutors and models of all Europe in the art of war, and then consider the fact that those very armies require now to be officered by foreign adventurers, in order to make them capable of even keeping together, and let him ask himself seriously, whether such a fall can ever be recovered. When, in the age of Theodosius, and again in that of Justinian, the Roman armies had fallen into the same state; when the Italian legions required to be led by Stilicho the Vandal, and the Byzantine by Belisar the Sclav and Narses the Persian, the end of all things was at hand, and came; as it will come soon to Turkey.

But if Turkey deserves to fall, and must fall, it must not fall by our treachery. Its sins will surely be avenged upon it: but wrong must not avenge wrong, or the penalty is only passed on from one sinner to another. Whatsoever element of good is left in the Turk, to that we must appeal as our only means, if not of saving him, still of helping him to a quiet euthanasia, and absorption into a worthier race of successors. He is said (I know not how truly) to have one virtue left; that of faithfulness to his word. Only by showing him that we too abhor treachery and bad faith, can we either do him good, or take a safe standing-ground in our own peril. And this we have done; and for this we shall be rewarded. But this is surely not all our duty. Even if we should be able to make the civil and religious freedom of the Eastern Christians the price of our assistance to the Mussulman, the struggle will not be over; for Russia will still be what she has always been, and the northern Anarch will be checked, only to return to the contest with fiercer lust of aggrandisement, to enact the part of a new Macedon, against a new Greece, divided, not united, by the treacherous bond of that balance of power, which is but war under the guise of peace. Europe needs a holier and more spiritual, and therefore a stronger union, than can be given by armed neutralities, and the so-called cause of order. She needs such a bond as in the Elizabethan age united the free states of Europe against the Anarch of Spain, and delivered the Western nations from a rising world-tyranny, which promised to be even more hideous than the elder one of Rome. If, as then, England shall proclaim herself the champion of freedom by acts, and not by words and paper, she may, as she did then, defy the rulers of the darkness of this world, for the God of Light will be with her. But, as yet, it is impossible to look without sad forebodings upon the destiny of a war, begun upon the express understanding that evil shall be left triumphant throughout Europe, wheresoever that evil does not seem, to our own selfish short-sightedness, to threaten us with immediate danger; with promises, that under the hollow name of the Cause of Order--and that promise made by a revolutionary Anarch--the wrongs of Italy, Hungary, Poland, Sweden, shall remain unredressed, and that Prussia and Austria, two tyrannies, the one far more false and hypocritical, the other even more rotten than that of Turkey, shall, if they will but observe a hollow and uncertain neutrality (for who can trust the liar and the oppressor?)--be allowed not only to keep their ill-gotten spoils, but even now to play into the hands of our foe, by guarding his Polish frontier for him, and keeping down the victims of his cruelty, under pretence of keeping down those of their own.

It is true, the alternative is an awful one; one from which statesmen and nations may well shrink: but it is a question, whether that alternative may not be forced upon us sooner or later, whether we must not from the first look it boldly in the face, as that which must be some day, and for which we must prepare, not cowardly, and with cries about God's wrath and judgments against us--which would be abject, were they not expressed in such second-hand stock-phrases as to make one altogether doubt their sincerity, but chivalrously, and with awful joy, as a noble calling, an honour put upon us by the God of Nations, who demands of us, as some small return for all His free bounties, that we should be, in this great crisis, the champions of Freedom and of Justice, which are the cause of God. At all events, we shall not escape our duty by being afraid of it; we shall not escape our duty by inventing to ourselves some other duty, and calling it "Order." Elizabeth did so at first. She tried to keep the peace with Spain; she shrank from injuring the cause of Order (then a nobler one than now, because it was the cause of Loyalty, and not merely of Mammon) by assisting the Scotch and the Netherlanders: but her duty was forced upon her; and she did it at last, cheerfully, boldly, utterly, like a hero; she put herself at the head of the battle for the freedom of the world, and she conquered, for God was with her; and so that seemingly most fearful of all England's perils, when the real meaning of it was seen, and God's will in it obeyed manfully, became the foundation of England's naval and colonial empire, and laid the foundation of all her future glories. So it was then, so it is now: so it will be for ever: he who seeks to save his life will lose it: he who willingly throws away his life for the cause of mankind, which is the cause of God, the Father of mankind, he shall save it, and be rewarded a hundred-fold. That God may grant us, the children of the Elizabethan heroes, all wisdom to see our duty, and courage to do it, even to the death, should be our earliest prayer. Our statesmen have done wisely and well in refusing, in spite of hot-headed clamours, to appeal to the sword as long as there was any chance of a peaceful settlement even of a single evil. They are doing wisely and well now in declining to throw away the scabbard as long as there is hope that a determined front will awe the offender into submission: but the day may come when the scabbard must be thrown away; and God grant that they may have the courage to do it.

It is reported that our rulers have said, that English diplomacy can no longer recognise "nationalities," but only existing "governments." God grant that they may see in time that the assertion of national life, as a spiritual and indefeasible existence, was for centuries the central idea of English policy; the idea by faith in which she delivered first herself, and then the Protestant nations of the Continent, successively from the yokes of Rome, of Spain, of France; and that they may reassert that most English of all truths again, let the apparent cost be what it may.

It is true, that this end will not be attained without what is called nowadays "a destruction of human life." But we have yet to learn (at least if the doctrines which I have tried to illustrate in this little book have any truth in them) whether shot or shell has the power of taking away human life; and to believe, if we believe our Bibles, that human life can only be destroyed by sin, and that all which is lost in battle is that animal life of which it is written, "Fear not those who can kill the body, and after that have no more that they can do: but I will forewarn you whom you shall fear; him who, after he has killed, has power to destroy both body and soul in hell." Let a man fear him, the destroying devil, and fear therefore cowardice, disloyalty, selfishness, sluggishness, which are his works, and to be utterly afraid of which is to be truly brave. God grant that we of the clergy may remember this during the coming war, and instead of weakening the righteous courage and honour of our countrymen by instilling into them selfish and superstitious fears, and a theory of the future state which represents God, not as a saviour, but a tormentor, may boldly tell them that "He is not the God of the dead but of the living; for all live unto Him;" and that he who renders up his animal life as a worthless thing, in the cause of duty, commits his real and human life, his very soul and self, into the hands of a just and merciful Father, who has promised to leave no good deed unrewarded, and least of all that most noble deed, the dying like a man for the sake not merely of this land of England, but of the freedom and national life of half the world.

LECTURE I--THE PTOLEMAIC ERA

Before I begin to lecture upon the Physical and Metaphysical schools of Alexandria, it may be better, perhaps, to define the meaning of these two epithets. Physical, we shall all agree, means that which belongs to [Greek text: phusis]; natura; nature, that which [Greek text: phuetai], nascitur, grows, by an organic life, and therefore decays again; which has a beginning, and therefore, I presume, an end. And Metaphysical means that which we learn to think of after we think of nature; that which is supernatural, in fact, having neither beginning nor end, imperishable, immovable, and eternal, which does not become, but always is. These, at least, are the wisest definitions of these two terms for us just now; for they are those which were received by the whole Alexandrian school, even by those commentators who say that Aristotle, the inventor of the term Metaphysics, named his treatise so only on account of its following in philosophic sequence his book on Physics.

But, according to these definitions, the whole history of Alexandria might be to us, from one point of view, a physical school; for Alexandria, its society and its philosophy, were born, and grew, and fed, and reached their vigour, and had their old age, their death, even as a plant or an animal has; and after they were dead and dissolved, the atoms of them formed food for new creations, entered into new organisations, just as the atoms of a dead plant or animal might do. Was Alexandria then, from beginning to end, merely a natural and physical phenomenon?

It may have been. And yet we cannot deny that Alexandria was also a metaphysical phenomenon, vast and deep enough; seeing that it held for some eighteen hundred years a population of several hundred thousand souls; each of whom, at least according to the Alexandrian philosophy, stood in a very intimate relation to those metaphysic things which are imperishable and immovable and eternal, and indeed, contained them more or less, each man, woman, and child of them in themselves; having wills, reasons, consciences, affections, relations to each other; being parents, children, helpmates, bound together by laws concerning right and wrong, and numberless other unseen and spiritual relations.

Surely such a body was not merely natural, any more than any other nation, society, or scientific school, made up of men and of the spirits, thoughts, affections of men. It, like them, was surely spiritual; and could be only living and healthy, in as far as it was in harmony with certain spiritual, unseen, and everlasting laws of God; perhaps, as certain Alexandrian philosophers would have held, in as far as it was a pattern of that ideal constitution and polity after which man was created, the city of God which is eternal in the Heavens. If so, may we not suspect of this Alexandria that it was its own fault if it became a merely physical phenomenon; and that it stooped to become a part of nature, and took its place among the things which are born to die, only by breaking the law which God had appointed for it; so fulfilling, in its own case, St. Paul's great words, that death entered into the world by sin, and that sin is the transgression of the law?

Be that as it may, there must have been metaphysic enough to be learnt in that, or any city of three hundred thousand inhabitants, even though it had never contained lecture-room or philosopher's chair, and had never heard the names of Aristotle and Plato. Metaphysic enough, indeed, to be learnt there, could we but enter into the heart of even the most brutish negro slave who ever was brought down the Nile out of the desert by Nubian merchants, to build piers and docks in whose commerce he did not share, temples whose worship he did not comprehend, libraries and theatres whose learning and civilisation were to him as much a sealed book as they were to his countryman, and fellow-slave, and only friend, the ape. There was metaphysic enough in him truly, and things eternal and immutable, though his dark-skinned descendants were three hundred years in discovering the fact, and in proving it satisfactorily to all mankind for ever. You must pardon me if I seem obscure; I cannot help looking at the question with a somewhat Alexandrian eye, and talking of the poor negro dock-worker as certain Alexandrian philosophers would have talked, of whom I shall have to speak hereafter.

I should have been glad, therefore, had time permitted me, instead of confining myself strictly to what are now called "the physic and metaphysic schools" of Alexandria, to have tried as well as I could to make you understand how the whole vast phenomenon grew up, and supported a peculiar life of its own, for fifteen hundred years and more, and was felt to be the third, perhaps the second city of the known world, and one so important to the great world-tyrant, the Caesar of Rome, that no Roman of distinction was ever sent there as prefect, but the Alexandrian national vanity and pride of race was allowed to the last to pet itself by having its tyrant chosen from its own people.

But, though this cannot be, we may find human elements enough in the schools of Alexandria, strictly so called, to interest us for a few evenings; for these schools were schools of men; what was discovered and taught was discovered and taught by men, and not by thinking-machines; and whether they would have been inclined to confess it or not, their own personal characters, likes and dislikes, hopes and fears, strength and weakness, beliefs and disbeliefs, determined their metaphysics and their physics for them, quite enough to enable us to feel for them as men of like passions with ourselves; and for that reason only, men whose thoughts and speculations are worthy of a moment's attention from us. For what is really interesting to man, save men, and God, the Father of men?

In the year 331 B.C. one of the greatest intellects whose influence the world has ever felt, saw, with his eagle glance, the unrivalled advantage of the spot which is now Alexandria; and conceived the mighty project of making it the point of union of two, or rather of three worlds. In a new city, named after himself, Europe, Asia, and Africa were to meet and to hold communion. A glance at the map will show you what an [Greek text: omphalosgees], a centre of the world, this Alexandria is, and perhaps arouse in your minds, as it has often done in mine, the suspicion that it has not yet fulfilled its whole destiny, but may become at any time a prize for contending nations, or the centre of some world-wide empire to come. Communicating with Europe and the Levant by the Mediterranean, with India by the Red Sea, certain of boundless supplies of food from the desert-guarded valley of the Nile, to which it formed the only key, thus keeping all Egypt, as it were, for its own private farm, it was weak only on one side, that of Judea. That small strip of fertile mountain land, containing innumerable military positions from which an enemy might annoy Egypt, being, in fact, one natural chain of fortresses, was the key to Phoenicia and Syria. It was an eagle's eyrie by the side of a pen of fowls. It must not be left defenceless for a single year. Tyre and Gaza had been taken; so no danger was to be apprehended from the seaboard: but to subdue the Judean mountaineers, a race whose past sufferings had hardened them in a dogged fanaticism of courage and endurance, would be a long and sanguinary task. It was better to make terms with them; to employ them as friendly warders of their own mountain walls. Their very fanaticism and isolation made them sure allies. There was no fear of their fraternising with the Eastern invaders. If the country was left in their hands, they would hold it against all comers. Terms were made with them; and for several centuries they fulfilled their trust.

This I apprehend to be the explanation of that conciliatory policy of Alexander's toward the Jews, which was pursued steadily by the Ptolemies, by Pompey, and by the Romans, as long as these same Jews continued to be endurable upon the face of the land. At least, we shall find the history of Alexandria and that of Judea inextricably united for more than three hundred years.

So arose, at the command of the great conqueror, a mighty city, around those two harbours, of which the western one only is now in use. The Pharos was then an island. It was connected with the mainland by a great mole, furnished with forts and drawbridges. On the ruins of that mole now stands the greater part of the modern city; the vast site of the ancient one is a wilderness.

But Alexander was not destined to carry out his own magnificent project. That was left for the general whom he most esteemed, and to whose personal prowess he had once owed his life; a man than whom history knows few greater, Ptolemy, the son of Lagus. He was an adventurer, the son of an adventurer, his mother a cast-off concubine of Philip of Macedon. There were those who said that he was in reality a son of Philip himself. However, he rose at court, became a private friend of young Alexander, and at last his Somatophylax, some sort of Colonel of the Life Guards. And from thence he rose rapidly, till after his great master's death he found himself despot of Egypt.

His face, as it appears on his coins, is of the loftiest and most Jove- like type of Greek beauty. There is a possibility about it, as about most old Greek faces, of boundless cunning; a lofty irony too, and a contemptuousness, especially about the mouth, which puts one in mind of Goethe's expression; the face, altogether, of one who knew men too well to respect them. At least, he was a man of clear enough vision. He saw what was needed in those strange times, and he went straight to the thing which he saw. It was his wisdom which perceived that the huge amorphous empire of Alexander could not be kept together, and advised its partition among the generals, taking care to obtain himself the lion's share; not in size, indeed, but in capability. He saw, too (what every man does not see), that the only way to keep what he had got was to make it better, and not worse, than he found it. His first Egyptian act was to put to death Cleomenes, Alexander's lieutenant, who had amassed vast treasures by extortion; and who was, moreover, (for Ptolemy was a prudent man) a dangerous partisan of his great enemy, Perdiccas. We do not read that he refunded the treasures: but the Egyptians surnamed him Soter, the Saviour; and on the whole he deserved the title. Instead of the wretched misrule and slavery of the conquering Persian dynasty, they had at least law and order, reviving commerce, and a system of administration, we are told (I confess to speaking here quite at second-hand), especially adapted to the peculiar caste-society, and the religious prejudices of Egypt. But Ptolemy's political genius went beyond such merely material and Warburtonian care for the conservation of body and goods of his subjects. He effected with complete success a feat which has been attempted, before and since, by very many princes and potentates, but has always, except in Ptolemy's case, proved somewhat of a failure, namely, the making a new deity. Mythology in general was in a rusty state. The old Egyptian gods had grown in his dominions very unfashionable, under the summary iconoclasm to which they had been subjected by the Monotheist Persians--the Puritans of the old world, as they have been well called. Indeed, all the dolls, and the treasure of the dolls' temples too, had been carried off by Cambyses to Babylon. And as for the Greek gods, philosophers had sublimed them away sadly during the last century: not to mention that Alexander's Macedonians, during their wanderings over the world, had probably become rather remiss in their religious exercises, and had possibly given up mentioning the Unseen world, except for those hortatory purposes for which it used to be employed by Nelson's veterans. But, as Ptolemy felt, people (women especially) must have something wherein to believe. The "Religious Sentiment" in man must be satisfied. But, how to do it? How to find a deity who would meet the aspirations of conquerors as well as conquered--of his most irreligious Macedonians, as well as of his most religious Egyptians? It was a great problem: but Ptolemy solved it. He seems to have taken the same method which Brindley the engineer used in his perplexities, for he went to bed. And there he had a dream: How the foreign god Serapis, of Pontus (somewhere near this present hapless Sinope), appeared to him, and expressed his wish to come to Alexandria, and there try his influence on the Religious Sentiment. So Serapis was sent for, and came--at least the idol of him, and-- accommodating personage!--he actually fitted. After he had been there awhile, he was found to be quite an old acquaintance--to be, in fact, the Greek Jove, and two or three other Greek gods, and also two or three Egyptian gods beside--indeed, to be no other than the bull Apis, after his death and deification. I can tell you no more. I never could find that anything more was known. You may see him among Greek and Roman statues as a young man, with a sort of high basket-shaped Persian turban on his head. But, at least, he was found so pleasant and accommodating a conscience-keeper, that he spread, with Isis, his newly-found mother, or wife, over the whole East, and even to Rome. The Consuls there--50 years B.C.--found the pair not too respectable, and pulled down their temples. But, so popular were they, in spite of their bad fame, that seven years after, the Triumvirs had to build the temples up again elsewhere; and from that time forth, Isis and Serapis, in spite, poor things, of much persecution, were the fashionable deities of the Roman world. Surely this Ptolemy was a man of genius!

But Ptolemy had even more important work to do than making gods. He had to make men; for he had few or none ready made among his old veterans from Issus and Arbela. He had no hereditary aristocracy: and he wanted none. No aristocracy of wealth; that might grow of itself, only too fast for his despotic power. But as a despot, he must have a knot of men round him who would do his work. And here came out his deep insight into fact. It had not escaped that man, what was the secret of Greek supremacy. How had he come there? How had his great master conquered half the world? How had the little semi-barbarous mountain tribe up there in Pella, risen under Philip to be the master-race of the globe? How, indeed, had Xenophon and his Ten Thousand, how had the handfuls of Salamis and Marathon, held out triumphantly century after century, against the vast weight of the barbarian? The simple answer was: Because the Greek has mind, the barbarian mere brute force. Because mind is the lord of matter; because the Greek being the cultivated man, is the only true man; the rest are [Greek text: barbaroi], mere things, clods, tools for the wise Greeks' use, in spite of all their material phantom-strength of elephants, and treasures, and tributaries by the million. Mind was the secret of Greek power; and for that Ptolemy would work. He would have an aristocracy of intellect; he would gather round him the wise men of the world (glad enough most of them to leave that miserable Greece, where every man's life was in his hand from hour to hour), and he would develop to its highest the conception of Philip, when he made Aristotle the tutor of his son Alexander. The consequences of that attempt were written in letters of blood, over half the world; Ptolemy would attempt it once more, with gentler results. For though he fought long, and often, and well, as Despot of Egypt, no less than as general of Alexander, he was not at heart a man of blood, and made peace the end of all his wars.

So he begins. Aristotle is gone: but in Aristotle's place Philetas the sweet singer of Cos, and Zenodotus the grammarian of Ephesus, shall educate his favourite son, and he will have a literary court, and a literary age. Demetrius Phalereus, the Admirable Crichton of his time, the last of Attic orators, statesman, philosopher, poet, warrior, and each of them in the most graceful, insinuating, courtly way, migrates to Alexandria, after having had the three hundred and sixty statues, which the Athenians had too hastily erected to his honour, as hastily pulled down again. Here was a prize for Ptolemy! The charming man became his bosom friend and fellow, even revised the laws of his kingdom, and fired him, if report says true, with a mighty thought--no less a one than the great public Library of Alexandria; the first such institution, it is said, which the world had ever seen.

So a library is begun by Soter, and organised and completed by Philadelphus; or rather two libraries, for while one part was kept at the Serapeium, that vast temple on the inland rising ground, of which, as far as we can discover, Pompey's Pillar alone remains, one column out of four hundred, the rest was in the Brucheion adjoining the Palace and the Museum. Philadelphus buys Aristotle's collection to add to the stock, and Euergetes cheats the Athenians out of the original MSS. of AEschylus, Sophocles, and Euripides, and adds largely to it by more honest methods. Eumenes, King of Pergamus in Asia Minor, fired with emulation, commences a similar collection, and is so successful, that the reigning Ptolemy has to cut off his rival's supplies by prohibiting the exportation of papyrus and the Pergamenian books are henceforth transcribed on parchment, parchemin, Pergamene, which thus has its name to this day, from Pergamus. That collection, too, found its way at last to Alexandria. For Antony having become possessor of it by right of the stronger, gave it to Cleopatra; and it remained at Alexandria for seven hundred years. But we must not anticipate events.

Then there must be besides a Mouseion, a Temple of the Muses, with all due appliances, in a vast building adjoining the palace itself, under the very wing of royalty; and it must have porticos, wherein sages may converse; lecture-rooms, where they may display themselves at their will to their rapt scholars, each like a turkey-cock before his brood; and a large dining-hall, where they may enjoy themselves in moderation, as befits sages, not without puns and repartees, epigrams, anagrams, and Attic salt, to be fatal, alas, to poor Diodorus the dialectician. For Stilpo, prince of sophists, having silenced him by some quibbling puzzle of logic, Ptolemy surnamed him Chronos the Slow. Poor Diodorus went home, took pen and ink, wrote a treatise on the awful nothing, and died in despair, leaving five "dialectical daughters" behind him, to be thorns in the sides of some five hapless men of Macedonia, as "emancipated women;" a class but too common in the later days of Greece, as they will always be, perhaps, in civilisations which are decaying and crumbling to pieces, leaving their members to seek in bewilderment what they are, and what bonds connect them with their fellow-beings. But to return: funds shall be provided for the Museum from the treasury; a priest of rank, appointed by royalty, shall be curator; botanical and zoological gardens shall be attached; collections of wonders made. In all things the presiding genius of Aristotle shall be worshipped; for these, like Alexander, were his pupils. Had he not mapped out all heaven and earth, things seen and unseen, with his entelechies, and energies, and dunameis, and put every created and uncreated thing henceforth into its proper place, from the ascidians and polypes of the sea to the virtues and the vices--yea, to that Great Deity and Prime Cause (which indeed was all things), Noesis Noeseon, "the Thought of Thoughts," whom he discovered by irrefragable processes of logic, and in whom the philosophers believe privately, leaving Serapis to the women and the sailors? All they had to do was to follow in his steps; to take each of them a branch, of science or literature, or as many branches as one man conveniently can; and working them out on the approved methods, end in a few years, as Alexander did, by weeping on the utmost shore of creation that there are no more worlds left to conquer.

Alas! the Muses are shy and wild; and though they will haunt, like skylarks, on the bleakest northern moor as cheerfully as on the sunny hills of Greece, and rise thence singing into the heaven of heavens, yet they are hard to tempt into a gilded cage, however amusingly made and plentifully stored with comforts. Royal societies, associations of savants, and the like, are good for many things, but not for the breeding of art and genius: for they are things which cannot be bred. Such institutions are excellent for physical science, when, as among us now, physical science is going on the right method: but where, as in Alexandria, it was going on an utterly wrong method, they stereotype the errors of the age, and invest them with the prestige of authority, and produce mere Sorbonnes, and schools of pedants. To literature, too, they do some good, that is, in a literary age--an age of reflection rather than of production, of antiquarian research, criticism, imitation, when book-making has become an easy and respectable pursuit for the many who cannot dig, and are ashamed to beg. And yet, by adding that same prestige of authority, not to mention of good society and Court favour, to the popular mania for literature, they help on the growing evil, and increase the multitude of prophets who prophesy out of their own heart and have seen nothing.

And this was, it must be said, the outcome of all the Ptolemaean appliances.

In Physics they did little. In Art nothing. In Metaphysics less than nothing.

We will first examine, as the more pleasant spectacle of the two, that branch of thought in which some progress was really made, and in which the Ptolemaic schools helped forward the development of men who have become world-famous, and will remain so, I suppose, until the end of time.

Four names at once attract us: Euclid, Aristarchus, Eratosthenes, Hipparchus. Archimedes, also, should be included in the list, for he was a pupil of the Alexandrian school, having studied (if Proclus is to be trusted) in Egypt, under Conon the Samian, during the reigns of two Ptolemies, Philadelphus and Euergetes.

Of Euclid, as the founder (according to Proclus) of the Alexandrian Mathematical school, I must of course speak first. Those who wish to attain to a juster conception of the man and his work than they can do from any other source, will do well to read Professor De Morgan's admirable article on him in "Smith's Classical Dictionary;" which includes, also, a valuable little sketch of the rise of Geometric science, from Pythagoras and Plato, of whose school Euclid was, to the great master himself.

I shall confine myself to one observation on Euclid's genius, and on the immense influence which it exerted on after generations. It seems to me, speaking under correction, that it exerted this, because it was so complete a type of the general tendency of the Greek mind, deductive, rather than inductive; of unrivalled subtlety in obtaining results from principles, and results again from them ad infinitum: deficient in that sturdy moral patience which is required for the examination of facts, and which has made Britain at once a land of practical craftsmen, and of earnest scientific discoverers.

Volatile, restless, "always children longing for something new," as the Egyptian priest said of them, they were too ready to believe that they had attained laws, and then, tired with their toy, throw away those hastily assumed laws, and wander off in search of others. Gifted, beyond all the sons of men, with the most exquisite perception of form, both physical and metaphysical, they could become geometers and logicians as they became sculptors and artists; beyond that they could hardly rise. The were conscious of their power to build; and it made them ashamed to dig.

Four men only among them seem, as far as I can judge, to have had a great inductive power: Socrates and Plato in Metaphysics; Archimedes and Hipparchus in Physics. But these men ran so far counter to the national genius, that their examples were not followed. As you will hear presently, the discoveries of Archimedes and Hipparchus were allowed to remain where they were for centuries. The Dialectic of Plato and Socrates was degraded into a mere art for making anything appear alternately true and false, and among the Megaric school, for undermining the ground of all science, and paving the way for scepticism, by denying the natural world to be the object of certain knowledge. The only element of Plato's thought to which they clung was, as we shall find from the Neoplatonists, his physical speculations; in which, deserting his inductive method, he has fallen below himself into the popular cacoethes, and Pythagorean deductive dreams about the mysterious powers of numbers, and of the regular solids.

Such a people, when they took to studying physical science, would be, and in fact were, incapable of Chemistry, Geognosy, Comparative Anatomy, or any of that noble choir of sister sciences, which are now building up the material as well as the intellectual glory of Britain.

To Astronomy, on the other hand, the pupils of Euclid turned naturally, as to the science which required the greatest amount of their favourite geometry: but even that they were content to let pass from its inductive to its deductive stage--not as we have done now, after two centuries of inductive search for the true laws, and their final discovery by Kepler and Newton: but as soon as Hipparchus had propounded any theory which would do instead of the true laws, content there to stop their experiments, and return to their favourite work of commenting, deducing, spinning notion out of notion, ad infinitum.

Still, they were not all of this temper. Had they been, they would have discovered, not merely a little, but absolutely nothing. For after all, if we will consider, induction being the right path to knowledge, every man, whether he knows it or not, uses induction, more or less, by the mere fact of his having a human reason, and knowing anything at all; as M. Jourdain talked prose all his life without being aware of it.

Aristarchus is principally famous for his attempt to discover the distance of the sun as compared with that of the moon. His method was ingenious enough, but too rough for success, as it depended principally on the belief that the line bounding the bright part of the moon was an exact straight line. The result was of course erroneous. He concluded that the sun was 18 times as far as the moon, and not, as we now know, 400; but his conclusion, like his conception of the vast extent of the sphere of the fixed stars, was far enough in advance of the popular doctrine to subject him, according to Plutarch, to a charge of impiety.

Eratosthenes, again, contributed his mite to the treasure of human science-- his one mite; and yet by that he is better known than by all the volumes which he seems to have poured out, on Ethics, Chronology, Criticism on the Old Attic Comedy, and what not, spun out of his weary brain during a long life of research and meditation. They have all perished,--like ninety-nine hundredths of the labours of that great literary age; and perhaps the world is no poorer for the loss. But one thing, which he attempted on a sound and practical philosophic method, stands, and will stand for ever. And after all, is not that enough to have lived for? to have found out one true thing, and, therefore, one imperishable thing, in one's life? If each one of us could but say when he died: "This one thing I have found out; this one thing I have proved to be possible; this one eternal fact I have rescued from Hela, the realm of the formless and unknown," how rich one such generation might make the world for ever!

But such is not the appointed method. The finders are few and far between, because the true seekers are few and far between; and a whole generation has often nothing to show for its existence but one solitary gem which some one man--often unnoticed in his time--has picked up for them, and so given them "a local habitation and a name."

Eratosthenes had heard that in Syene, in Upper Egypt, deep wells were enlightened to the bottom on the day of the summer solstice, and that vertical objects cast no shadows.

He had before suggested, as is supposed, to Ptolemy Euergetes, to make him the two great copper armillae, or circles for determining the equinox, which stood for centuries in "that which is called the Square Porch"--probably somewhere in the Museum. By these he had calculated the obliquity of the ecliptic, closely enough to serve for a thousand years after. That was one work done. But what had the Syene shadows to do with that? Syene must be under that ecliptic. On the edge of it. In short, just under the tropic. Now he had ascertained exactly the latitude of one place on the earth's surface. He had his known point from whence to start on a world-journey, and he would use it; he would calculate the circumference of the earth--and he did it. By observations made at Alexandria, he ascertained its latitude compared with that of Syene; and so ascertained what proportion to the whole circumference was borne by the 5000 stadia between Alexandria and Syene. He fell into an error, by supposing Alexandria and Syene to be under the same meridians of longitude: but that did not prevent his arriving at a fair rough result of 252,000 stadia--31,500 Roman miles; considerably too much; but still, before him, I suppose, none knew whether it was 10,000, or 10,000,000. The right method having once been found, nothing remained but to employ it more accurately.

One other great merit of Eratosthenes is, that he first raised Geography to the rank of a science. His Geographica were an organic collection, the first the world had ever seen, of all the travels and books of earth-description heaped together in the Great Library, of which he was for many years the keeper. He began with a geognostic book, touched on the traces of Cataclysms and Change visible on the earth's surface; followed by two books, one a mathematical book, the other on political geography, and completed by a map--which one would like to see: but-- not a trace of all remains, save a few quoted fragments -

We are such stuff As dreams are made of.

But if Eratosthenes had hold of eternal fact and law on one point, there was a contemporary who had hold of it in more than one. I mean Archimedes; of whom, as I have said, we must speak as of an Alexandrian. It was as a mechanician, rather than as an astronomer, that he gained his reputation. The stories of his Hydraulic Screw, the Great Ship which he built for Hiero, and launched by means of machinery, his crane, his war-engines, above all his somewhat mythical arrangement of mirrors, by which he set fire to ships in the harbour--all these, like the story of his detecting the alloy in Hiero's crown, while he himself was in the bath, and running home undressed shouting [Greek text: eureeka]--all these are schoolboys' tales. To the thoughtful person it is the method of the man which constitutes his real greatness, that power of insight by which he solved the two great problems of the nature of the lever and of hydrostatic pressure, which form the basis of all static and hydrostatic science to this day. And yet on that very question of the lever the great mind of Aristotle babbles--neither sees the thing itself, nor the way towards seeing it. But since Archimedes spoke, the thing seems self-evident to every schoolboy. There is something to me very solemn in such a fact as this. It brings us down to some of the very deepest questions of metaphysic. This mental insight of which we boast so much, what is it? Is it altogether a process of our own brain and will? If it be, why have so few the power, even among men of power, and they so seldom? If brain alone were what was wanted, what could not Aristotle have discovered? Or is it that no man can see a thing unless God shows it him? Is it that in each separate act of induction, that mysterious and transcendental process which cannot, let logicians try as they will, be expressed by any merely logical formula, Aristotelian or other--is it I say, that in each separate act of induction we do not find the law, but the law is shown to us, by Him who made the law? Bacon thought so. Of that you may find clear proof in his writings. May not Bacon be right? May it not be true that God does in science, as well as in ethics, hide things from the wise and prudent, from the proud, complete, self-contained systematiser like Aristotle, who must needs explain all things in heaven and earth by his own formulae, and his entelechies and energies, and the rest of the notions which he has made for himself out of his own brain, and then pack each thing away in its proper niche in his great cloud-universe of conceptions? Is it that God hides things from such men many a time, and reveals them to babes, to gentle, affectionate, simple-hearted men, such as we know Archimedes to have been, who do not try to give an explanation for a fact, but feel how awful and divine it is, and wrestle reverently and stedfastly with it, as Jacob with the Angel, and will not let it go, until it bless them? Sure I am, from what I have seen of scientific men, that there is an intimate connection between the health of the moral faculties and the health of the inductive ones; and that the proud, self-conceited, and passionate man will see nothing: perhaps because nothing will be shown him.

But we must leave Archimedes for a man not perhaps so well known, but to whom we owe as much as to the great Syracusan--Hipparchus the astronomer. To his case much which I have just said applies. In him astronomic science seemed to awaken suddenly to a true inductive method, and after him to fall into its old slumber for 300 years. In the meantime Timocharis, Aristyllus, and Conon had each added their mites to the discoveries of Eratosthenes: but to Hipparchus we owe that theory of the heavens, commonly called the Ptolemaic system, which, starting from the assumption that the earth was the centre of the universe, attempted to explain the motions of the heavenly bodies by a complex system of supposed eccentrics and epicycles. This has of course now vanished before modern discoveries. But its value as a scientific attempt lies in this: that the method being a correct one, correct results were obtained, though starting from a false assumption; and Hipparchus and his successors were enabled by it to calculate and predict the changes of the heavens, in spite of their clumsy instruments, with almost as much accuracy as we do now.

For the purpose of working out this theory he required a science of trigonometry, plane and spherical: and this he accordingly seems to have invented. To him also we owe the discovery of that vast gradual change in the position of the fixed stars, in fact, of the whole celestial system, now known by the name of the precession of the equinoxes; the first great catalogue of fixed stars, to the number of 1080; attempts to ascertain whether the length of years and days were constant; with which, with his characteristic love of truth, he seems to have been hardly satisfied. He too invented the planisphere, or mode of representing the starry heavens upon a plane, and is the father of true geography, having formed the happy notion of mapping out the earth, as well as the heavens, by degrees of latitude and longitude.

Strange it is, and somewhat sad, that we should know nothing of this great man, should be hardly able to distinguish him from others of the same name, but through the works of a commentator, who wrote and observed in Alexandria 300 years after, during the age of the Antonines. I mean, of course, the famous Ptolemy, whose name so long bore the honour of that system which really belonged to Hipparchus.

This single fact speaks volumes for the real weakness of the great artificial school of literature and science founded by the kings of Egypt. From the father of Astronomy, as Delambre calls him, to Ptolemy, the first man who seems really to have appreciated him, we have not a discovery, hardly an observation or a name, to fill the gap. Physical sages there were; but they were geometers and mathematicians, rather than astronomic observers and inquirers. And in spite of all the huge appliances and advantages of that great Museum, its inhabitants were content, in physical science, as in all other branches of thought, to comment, to expound, to do everything but open their eyes and observe facts, and learn from them, as the predecessors whom they pretended to honour had done. But so it is always. A genius, an original man appears. He puts himself boldly in contact with facts, asks them what they mean, and writes down their answer for the world's use. And then his disciples must needs form a school, and a system; and fancy that they do honour to their master by refusing to follow in his steps; by making his book a fixed dogmatic canon; attaching to it some magical infallibility; declaring the very lie which he disproved by his whole existence, that discovery is henceforth impossible, and the sum of knowledge complete: instead of going on to discover as he discovered before them, and in following his method, show that they honour him, not in the letter, but in spirit and in truth.

For this, if you will consider, is the true meaning of that great command, "Honour thy father and mother, that thy days may be long in the land." On reverence for the authority of bygone generations depends the permanence of every form of thought or belief, as much as of all social, national, and family life: but on reverence of the spirit, not merely of the letter; of the methods of our ancestors, not merely of their conclusions. Ay, and we shall not be able to preserve their conclusions, not even to understand them; they will die away on our lips into skeleton notions, and soulless phrases, unless we see that the greatness of the mighty dead has always consisted in this, that they were seekers, improvers, inventors, endued with that divine power and right of discovery which has been bestowed on us, even as on them; unless we become such men as they were, and go on to cultivate and develop the precious heritage which they have bequeathed to us, instead of hiding their talent in a napkin and burying it in the earth; making their greatness an excuse for our own littleness, their industry for our laziness, their faith for our despair; and prating about the old paths, while we forget that paths were made that men might walk in them, and not stand still, and try in vain to stop the way.

It may be said, certainly, as an excuse for these Alexandrian Greeks, that they were a people in a state of old age and decay; and that they only exhibited the common and natural faults of old age. For as with individuals, so with races, nations, societies, schools of thought-- youth is the time of free fancy and poetry; manhood of calm and strong induction; old age of deduction, when men settle down upon their lees, and content themselves with reaffirming and verifying the conclusions of their earlier years, and too often, alas! with denying and anathematising all conclusions which have been arrived at since their own meridian. It is sad: but it is patent and common. It is sad to think that the day may come to each of us, when we shall have ceased to hope for discovery and for progress; when a thing will seem e priori false to us, simply because it is new; and we shall be saying querulously to the Divine Light which lightens every man who comes into the world: "Hitherto shalt thou come, and no further. Thou hast taught men enough; yea rather, thou hast exhausted thine own infinitude, and hast no more to teach them." Surely such a temper is to be fought against, prayed against, both in ourselves, and in the generation in which we live. Surely there is no reason why such a temper should overtake old age. There may be reason enough, "in the nature of things." For that which is of nature is born only to decay and die. But in man there is more than dying nature; there is spirit, and a capability of spiritual and everlasting life, which renews its youth like the eagle's, and goes on from strength to strength, and which, if it have its autumns and its winters, has no less its ever-recurring springs and summers; if it has its Sabbaths, finds in them only rest and refreshment for coming labour. And why not in nations, societies, scientific schools? These too are not merely natural: they are spiritual, and are only living and healthy in as far as they are in harmony with spiritual, unseen, and everlasting laws of God. May not they, too, have a capability of everlasting life, as long as they obey those laws in faith, and patience, and humility? We cannot deny the analogy between the individual man and these societies of men. We cannot, at least, deny the analogy between them in growth, decay, and death. May we not have hope that it holds good also for that which can never die; and that if they do die, as this old Greek society did, it is by no brute natural necessity, but by their own unfaithfulness to that which they knew, to that which they ought to have known? It is always more hopeful, always, as I think, more philosophic, to throw the blame of failure on man, on our own selves, rather than on God, and the perfect law of His universe. At least let us be sure for ourselves, that such an old age as befell this Greek society, as befalls many a man nowadays, need not be our lot. Let us be sure that earth shows no fairer sight than the old man, whose worn-out brain and nerves make it painful, and perhaps impossible, to produce fresh thought himself: but who can yet welcome smilingly and joyfully the fresh thoughts of others; who keeps unwearied his faith in God's government of the universe, in God's continual education of the human race; who draws around him the young and the sanguine, not merely to check their rashness by his wise cautions, but to inspirit their sloth by the memories of his own past victories; who hands over, without envy or repining, the lamp of truth to younger runners than himself, and sits contented by, bidding the new generation God speed along the paths untrodden by him, but seen afar off by faith. A few such old persons have I seen, both men and women; in whom the young heart beat pure and fresh, beneath the cautious and practised brain of age, and gray hairs which were indeed a crown of glory. A few such have I seen; and from them I seemed to learn what was the likeness of our Father who is in heaven. To such an old age may He bring you and me, and all for whom we are bound to pray.

LECTURE II--THE PTOLEMAIC ERA (Continued.)

I said in my first Lecture, that even if royal influence be profitable for the prosecution of physical science, it cannot be profitable for art. It can only produce a literary age, as it did in the Ptolemaic era; a generation of innumerable court-poets, artificial epigrammatists, artificial idyllists, artificial dramatists and epicists; above all, a generation of critics. Or rather shall we say, that the dynasty was not the cause of a literary age, but only its correlative? That when the old Greeks lost the power of being free, of being anything but the slaves of oriental despots, as the Ptolemies in reality were, they lost also the power of producing true works of art; because they had lost that youthful vigour of mind from which both art and freedom sprang? Let the case be as it will, Alexandrian literature need not detain us long--though, alas! it has detained every boy who ever trembled over his Greek grammar, for many a weary year; and, I cannot help suspecting, has been the main cause that so many young men who have spent seven years in learning Greek, know nothing about it at the end of the seven. For I must say, that as far as we can see, these Alexandrian pedants were thorough pedants; very polished and learned gentlemen, no doubt, and, like Callimachus, the pets of princes: but after all, men who thought that they could make up for not writing great works themselves, by showing, with careful analysis and commentation, how men used to write them of old, or rather how they fancied men used to write them; for, consider, if they had really known how the thing was done, they must needs have been able to do it themselves. Thus Callimachus, the favourite of Ptolemy Philadelphus, and librarian of his Museum, is the most distinguished grammarian, critic, and poet of his day, and has for pupils Eratosthenes, Apollonius Rhodius, Aristophanes of Byzantium, and a goodly list more. He is an encyclopaedia in himself. There is nothing the man does not know, or probably, if we spoke more correctly, nothing he does not know about. He writes on history, on the Museum, on barbarous names, on the wonders of the world, on public games, on colonisation, on winds, on birds, on the rivers of the world, and-- ominous subject--a sort of comprehensive history of Greek literature, with a careful classification of all authors, each under his own heading. Greek literature was rather in the sere and yellow leaf, be sure, when men thought of writing that sort of thing about it. But still, he is an encyclopaedic man, and, moreover, a poet. He writes an epic, "Aitia," in four books, on the causes of the myths, religious ceremonies, and so forth--an ominous sign for the myths also, and the belief in them; also a Hecate, Galataea, Glaucus--four epics, besides comedies, tragedies, iambics, choriambics, elegies, hymns, epigrams seventy-three--and of these last alone can we say that they are in any degree readable; and they are courtly, far-fetched, neat, and that is all. Six hymns remain, and a few fragments of the elegies: but the most famous elegy, on Berenice's hair, is preserved to us only in a Latin paraphrase of Catullus. It is curious, as the earliest instance we have of genuinely ungenuine Court poetry, and of the complimentary lie which does not even pretend to be true; the flattery which will not take the trouble to prevent your seeing that it is laughing in your face.

Berenice the queen, on Ptolemy's departure to the wars, vows her beautiful tresses to her favourite goddess, as the price of her husband's safe return; and duly pays her vow. The hair is hung up in the temple: in a day or two after it has vanished. Dire is the wrath of Ptolemy, the consternation of the priests, the scandal to religion; when Conon, the court-astronomer, luckily searching the heavens, finds the missing tresses in an utterly unexpected place--as a new constellation of stars, which to this day bears the title of Coma Berenices. It is so convenient to believe the fact, that everybody believes it accordingly; and Callimachus writes an elegy thereon, in which the constellified, or indeed deified tresses, address in most melodious and highly-finished Greek, bedizened with concetto on concetto, that fair and sacred head whereon they grew, to be shorn from which is so dire a sorrow, that apotheosis itself can hardly reconcile them to the parting.

Worthy, was not all this, of the descendants of the men who fought at Marathon and Thermopylae? The old Greek civilisation was rotting swiftly down; while a fire of God was preparing, slowly and dimly, in that unnoticed Italian town of Rome, which was destined to burn up that dead world, and all its works.

Callimachus's hymns, those may read who list. They are highly finished enough; the work of a man who knew thoroughly what sort of article he intended to make, and what were the most approved methods of making it. Curious and cumbrous mythological lore comes out in every other line. The smartness, the fine epithets, the recondite conceits, the bits of effect, are beyond all praise; but as for one spark of life, of poetry, of real belief, you will find none; not even in that famous Lavacrum Palladis which Angelo Poliziano thought worth translating into Latin elegiacs, about the same time that the learned Florentine, Antonio Maria Salviano, found Berenice's Hair worthy to be paraphrased back from Catullus' Latin into Greek, to give the world some faint notion of the inestimable and incomparable original. They must have had much time on their hands. But at the Revival of Letters, as was to be expected, all works of the ancients, good and bad, were devoured alike with youthful eagerness by the Medicis and the Popes; and it was not, we shall see, for more than one century after, that men's taste got sufficiently matured to distinguish between Callimachus and the Homeric hymns, or between Plato and Proclus. Yet Callimachus and his fellows had an effect on the world. His writings, as well as those of Philetas, were the model on which Ovid, Propertius, Tibullus, formed themselves.

And so I leave him, with two hints. If any one wishes to see the justice of my censure, let him read one of the Alexandrian hymns, and immediately after it, one of those glorious old Homeric hymns to the very same deities; let him contrast the insincere and fulsome idolatry of Callimachus with the reverent, simple and manful anthropomorphism of the Homerist--and let him form his own judgment.

The other hint is this. If Callimachus, the founder of Alexandrian literature, be such as he is, what are his pupils likely to become, at least without some infusion of healthier blood, such as in the case of his Roman imitators produced a new and not altogether ignoble school?

Of Lycophron, the fellow-grammarian and poet of Callimachus, we have nothing left but the Cassandra, a long iambic poem, stuffed with traditionary learning, and so obscure, that it obtained for him the surname of [Greek text: skoteinos] the dark one. I have tried in vain to read it: you, if you will, may do the same.

Philetas, the remaining member of the Alexandrian Triad, seems to have been a more simple, genial, and graceful spirit than the other two, to whom he was accordingly esteemed inferior. Only a few fragments are left; but he was not altogether without his influence, for he was, as I have just said, one of the models on which Propertius and Ovid formed themselves; and some, indeed, call him the Father of the Latin elegy, with its terseness, grace, and clear epigrammatic form of thought, and, therefore, in a great degree, of our modern eighteenth century poets; not a useless excellence, seeing that it is, on the whole, good for him who writes to see clearly what he wants to say, and to be able to make his readers see it clearly also. And yet one natural strain is heard amid all this artificial jingle--that of Theocritus. It is not altogether Alexandrian. Its sweetest notes were learnt amid the chestnut groves and orchards, the volcanic glens and sunny pastures of Sicily; but the intercourse, between the courts of Hiero and the Ptolemies seems to have been continual. Poets and philosophers moved freely from one to the other, and found a like atmosphere in both; and in one of Theocritus' idyls, two Sicilian gentlemen, crossed in love, agree to sail for Alexandria, and volunteer into the army of the great and good king Ptolemy, of whom a sketch is given worth reading; as a man noble, generous, and stately, "knowing well who loves him, and still better who loves him not." He has another encomium on Ptolemy, more laboured, though not less interesting: but the real value of Theocritus lies in his power of landscape-painting.

One can well conceive the delight which his idyls must have given to those dusty Alexandrians, pent up forever between sea and sand-hills, drinking the tank-water, and never hearing the sound of a running stream--whirling, too, forever, in all the bustle and intrigue of a great commercial and literary city. Refreshing indeed it must have been to them to hear of those simple joys and simple sorrows of the Sicilian shepherd, in a land where toil was but exercise, and mere existence was enjoyment. To them, and to us also. I believe Theocritus is one of the poets who will never die. He sees men and things, in his own light way, truly; and he describes them simply, honestly, with little careless touches of pathos and humour, while he floods his whole scene with that gorgeous Sicilian air, like one of Titian's pictures; with still sunshine, whispering pines, the lizard sleeping on the wall, and the sun-burnt cicala shrieking on the spray, the pears and apples dropping from the orchard bough, the goats clambering from crag to crag after the cistus and the thyme, the brown youths and wanton lasses singing under the dark chestnut boughs, or by the leafy arch of some

Grot nymph-haunted, Garlanded over with vine, and acanthus, and clambering roses, Cool in the fierce still noon, where the streams glance clear in the moss-beds;

and here and there, beyond the braes and meads, blue glimpses of the far-off summer sea; and all this told in a language and a metre which shapes itself almost unconsciously, wave after wave, into the most luscious song. Doubt not that many a soul then, was the simpler, and purer, and better, for reading the sweet singer of Syracuse. He has his immoralities; but they are the immoralities of his age: his naturalness, his sunny calm and cheerfulness, are all his own.

And now, to leave the poets, and speak of those grammarians to whose corrections we owe, I suppose, the texts of the Greek poets as they now stand. They seem to have set to work at their task methodically enough, under the direction of their most literary monarch, Ptolemy Philadelphus. Alexander the AEtolian collected and revised the tragedies, Lycophron the comedies, Zenodctus the poems of Homer, and the other poets of the Epic cycle, now lost to us. Whether Homer prospered under all his expungings, alterations, and transpositions--whether, in fact, he did not treat Homer very much as Bentley wanted to treat Milton, is a suspicion which one has a right to entertain, though it is long past the possibility of proof. Let that be as it may, the critical business grew and prospered. Aristophanes of Byzantium wrote glossaries and grammars, collected editions of Plato and Aristotle, aesthetic disquisitions on Homer--one wishes they were preserved, for the sake of the jest, that one might have seen an Alexandrian cockney's views of Achilles and Ulysses! Moreover, in a hapless moment, at least for us moderns, he invented Greek accents; thereby, I fear, so complicating and confusing our notions of Greek rhythm, that we shall never, to the end of time, be able to guess what any Greek verse, saving the old Homeric Hexameter, sounded like. After a while, too, the pedants, according to their wont, began quarrelling about their accents and their recessions. Moreover, there was a rival school at Pergamus where the fame of Crates all but equalled the Egyptian fame of Aristarchus. Insolent! What right had an Asiatic to know anything? So Aristarchus flew furiously on Crates, being a man of plain common sense, who felt a correct reading a far more important thing than any of Crates's illustrations, aesthetic, historical, or mythological; a preference not yet quite extinct, in one, at least, of our Universities. "Sir," said a clever Cambridge Tutor to a philosophically inclined freshman, "remember, that our business is to translate Plato correctly, not to discover his meaning." And, paradoxical as it may seem, he was right. Let us first have accuracy, the merest mechanical accuracy, in every branch of knowledge. Let us know what the thing is which we are looking at. Let us know the exact words an author uses. Let us get at the exact value of each word by that severe induction of which Buttmann and the great Germans have set such noble examples; and then, and not till then, we may begin to talk about philosophy, and aesthetics, and the rest. Very Probably Aristarchus was right in his dislike of Crates's preference of what he called criticism, to grammar. Very probably he connected it with the other object of his especial hatred, that fashion of interpreting Homer allegorically, which was springing up in his time, and which afterwards under the Neoplatonists rose to a frantic height, and helped to destroy in them, not only their power of sound judgment, and of asking each thing patiently what it was, but also any real reverence for, or understanding of, the very authors over whom they declaimed and sentimentalised.

Yes--the Cambridge Tutor was right. Before you can tell what a man means, you must have patience to find out what he says. So far from wishing our grammatical and philological education to be less severe than it is, I think it is not severe enough. In an age like this--an age of lectures, and of popular literature, and of self-culture, too often random and capricious, however earnest, we cannot be too careful in asking ourselves, in compelling others to ask themselves, the meaning of every word which they use, of every word which they read; in assuring them, whether they will believe us or not, that the moral, as well as the intellectual culture, acquired by translating accurately one dialogue of Plato, by making out thoroughly the sense of one chapter of a standard author, is greater than they will get from skimming whole folios of Schlegelian aesthetics, resumes, histories of philosophy, and the like second-hand information, or attending seven lectures a-week till their lives' end. It is better to know one thing, than to know about ten thousand things. I cannot help feeling painfully, after reading those most interesting Memoirs of Margaret Fuller Ossoli, that the especial danger of this time is intellectual sciolism, vagueness, sentimental eclecticism--and feeling, too, as Socrates of old believed, that intellectual vagueness and shallowness, however glib, and grand, and eloquent it may seem, is inevitably the parent of a moral vagueness and shallowness, which may leave our age as it left the later Greeks, without an absolute standard of right or of truth, till it tries to escape from its own scepticism, as the later Neoplatonists did, by plunging desperately into any fetish-worshipping superstition which holds out to its wearied and yet impatient intellect, the bait of decisions already made for it, of objects of admiration already formed and systematised.

Therefore let us honour the grammarian in his place; and, among others, these old grammarians of Alexandria; only being sure that as soon as any man begins, as they did, displaying himself peacock-fashion, boasting of his science as the great pursuit of humanity, and insulting his fellow- craftsmen, he becomes, ipso facto, unable to discover any more truth for us, having put on a habit of mind to which induction is impossible; and is thenceforth to be passed by with a kindly but a pitying smile. And so, indeed, it happened with these quarrelsome Alexandrian grammarians, as it did with the Casaubons and Scaligers and Daciers of the last two centuries. As soon as they began quarrelling they lost the power of discovering. The want of the inductive faculty in their attempts at philology is utterly ludicrous. Most of their derivations of words are about on a par with Jacob Bohmen's etymology of sulphur, wherein he makes sul, if I recollect right, signify some active principle of combustion, and phur the passive one. It was left for more patient and less noisy men, like Grimm, Bopp, and Buttmann, to found a science of philology, to discover for us those great laws which connect modern philology with history, ethnology, physiology, and with the very deepest questions of theology itself. And in the meanwhile, these Alexandrians' worthless criticism has been utterly swept away; while their real work, their accurate editions of the classics, remain to us as a precious heritage. So it is throughout history: nothing dies which is worthy to live. The wheat is surely gathered into the garner, the chaff is burnt up by that eternal fire which, happily for this universe, cannot be quenched by any art of man, but goes on forever, devouring without indulgence all the folly and the falsehood of the world.

As yet you have heard nothing of the metaphysical schools of Alexandria; for as yet none have existed, in the modern acceptation of that word. Indeed, I am not sure that I must not tell you frankly, that none ever existed at all in Alexandria, in that same modern acceptation. Ritter, I think, it is who complains naively enough, that the Alexandrian Neoplatonists had a bad habit, which grew on them more and more as the years rolled on, of mixing up philosophy with theology, and so defiling, or at all events colouring, its pure transparency. There is no denying the imputation, as I shall show at greater length in my next Lecture. But one would have thought, looking back through history, that the Alexandrians were not the only philosophers guilty of this shameful act of syncretism. Plato, one would have thought, was as great a sinner as they. So were the Hindoos. In spite of all their logical and metaphysical acuteness, they were, you will find, unable to get rid of the notion that theological inquiries concerning Brahma, Atma, Creeshna, were indissolubly mixed up with that same logic and metaphysic. The Parsees could not separate questions about Ahriman and Ormuzd from Kant's three great philosophic problems: What is Man?--What may be known?--What should be done? Neither, indeed, could the earlier Greek sages. Not one of them, of any school whatsoever--from the semi-mythic Seven Sages to Plato and Aristotle--but finds it necessary to consider not in passing, but as the great object of research, questions concerning the gods:- whether they are real or not; one or many; personal or impersonal; cosmic, and parts of the universe, or organisers and rulers of it; in relation to man, or without relation to him. Even in those who flatly deny the existence of the gods, even in Lucretius himself, these questions have to be considered, before the question, What is man? can get any solution at all. On the answer given to them is found to depend intimately the answer to the question, What is the immaterial part of man? Is it a part of nature, or of something above nature? Has he an immaterial part at all?--in one word, Is a human metaphysic possible at all? So it was with the Greek philosophers of old, even, as Asclepius and Ammonius say, with Aristotle himself. "The object of Aristotle's metaphysic," one of them says, "is theological. Herein Aristotle theologises." And there is no denying the assertion. We must not then be hard on the Neoplatonists, as if they were the first to mix things separate from the foundation of the world. I do not say that theology and metaphysic are separate studies. That is to be ascertained only by seeing some one separate them. And when I see them separated, I shall believe them separable. Only the separation must not be produced by the simple expedient of denying the existence of either one of them, or at least of ignoring the existence of one steadily during the study of the other. If they can be parted without injury to each other, let them be parted; and till then let us suspend hard judgments on the Alexandrian school of metaphysic, and also on the schools of that curious people the Jews, who had at this period a steadily increasing influence on the thought, as well as on the commercial prosperity, of Alexandria.

You must not suppose, in the meanwhile, that the philosophers whom the Ptolemies collected (as they would have any other marketable article) by liberal offers of pay and patronage, were such men as the old Seven Sages of Greece, or as Socrates, Plato, and Aristotle. In these three last indeed, Greek thought reached not merely its greatest height, but the edge of a precipice down which it rolled headlong after their decease. The intellectual defects of the Greek mind, of which I have already spoken, were doubtless one great cause of this decay: but, to my mind, moral causes had still more to do with it. The more cultivated Greek states, to judge from the writings of Plato, had not been an over- righteous people during the generation in which he lived. And in the generations which followed, they became an altogether wicked people; immoral, unbelieving, hating good, and delighting in all which was evil. And it was in consequence of these very sins of theirs, as I think, that the old Hellenic race began to die out physically, and population throughout Greece to decrease with frightful rapidity, after the time of the Achaean league. The facts are well known; and foul enough they are. When the Romans destroyed Greece, God was just and merciful. The eagles were gathered together only because the carrion needed to be removed from the face of God's earth. And at the time of which I now speak, the signs of approaching death were fearfully apparent. Hapless and hopeless enough were the clique of men out of whom the first two Ptolemies hoped to form a school of philosophy; men certainly clever enough, and amusing withal, who might give the kings of Egypt many a shrewd lesson in king-craft, and the ways of this world, and the art of profiting by the folly of fools, and the selfishness of the selfish; or who might amuse them, in default of fighting-cocks, by puns and repartees, and battles of logic; "how one thing cannot be predicated of another," or "how the wise man is not only to overcome every misfortune, but not even to feel it," and other such mighty questions, which in those days hid that deep unbelief in any truth whatsoever which was spreading fast over the minds of men. Such word-splitters were Stilpo and Diodorus, the slayer and the slain. They were of the Megaran school, and were named Dialectics; and also, with more truth, Eristics, or quarrellers. Their clique had professed to follow Zeno and Socrates in declaring the instability of sensible presumptions and conclusions, in preaching an absolute and eternal Being. But there was this deep gulf between them and Socrates; that while Socrates professed to be seeking for the Absolute and Eternal, for that which is, they were content with affirming that it exists. With him, as with the older sages, philosophy was a search for truth. With them it was a scheme of doctrines to be defended. And the dialectic on which they prided themselves so much, differed from his accordingly. He used it inductively, to seek out, under the notions and conceptions of the mind, certain absolute truths and laws of which they were only the embodiment. Words and thought were to him a field for careful and reverent induction, as the phenomena of nature are to us the disciples of Bacon. But with these hapless Megarans, who thought that they had found that for which Socrates professed only to seek dimly and afar off, and had got it safe in a dogma, preserved as it were in spirits, and put by in a museum, the great use of dialectic was to confute opponents. Delight in their own subtlety grew on them, the worship not of objective truth, but of the forms of the intellect whereby it may be demonstrated; till they became the veriest word-splitters, rivals of the old sophists whom their master had attacked, and justified too often Aristophanes' calumny, which confounded Socrates with his opponents, as a man whose aim was to make the worse appear the better reason.

We have here, in both parties, all the marks of an age of exhaustion, of scepticism, of despair about finding any real truth. No wonder that they were superseded by the Pyrrhonists, who doubted all things, and by the Academy, which prided itself on setting up each thing to knock it down again; and so by prudent and well-bred and tolerant qualifying of every assertion, neither affirming too much, nor denying too much, keep their minds in a wholesome--or unwholesome--state of equilibrium, as stagnant pools are kept, that everything may have free toleration to rot undisturbed.

These hapless caricaturists of the dialectic of Plato, and the logic of Aristotle, careless of any vital principles or real results, ready enough to use fallacies each for their own party, and openly proud of their success in doing so, were assisted by worthy compeers of an outwardly opposite tone of thought, the Cyrenaics, Theodorus and Hegesias. With their clique, as with their master Aristippus, the senses were the only avenues to knowledge; man was the measure of all things; and "happiness our being's end and aim." Theodorus was surnamed the Atheist; and, it seems, not without good reason; for he taught that there was no absolute or eternal difference between good and evil; nothing really disgraceful in crimes; no divine ground for laws, which according to him had been invented by men to prevent fools from making themselves disagreeable; on which theory, laws must be confessed to have been in all ages somewhat of a failure. He seems to have been, like his master, an impudent light-hearted fellow, who took life easily enough, laughed at patriotism, and all other high-flown notions, boasted that the world was his country, and was no doubt excellent after-dinner company for the great king. Hegesias, his fellow Cyrenaic, was a man of a darker and more melancholic temperament; and while Theodorus contented himself with preaching a comfortable selfishness, and obtaining pleasure, made it rather his study to avoid pain. Doubtless both their theories were popular enough at Alexandria, as they were in France during the analogous period, the Siecle Louis Quinze. The "Contrat Social," and the rest of their doctrines, moral and metaphysical, will always have their admirers on earth, as long as that variety of the human species exists for whose especial behoof Theodorus held that laws were made; and the whole form of thought met with great approbation in after years at Rome, where Epicurus carried it to its highest perfection. After that, under the pressure of a train of rather severe lessons, which Gibbon has detailed in his "Decline and Fall of the Roman Empire," little or nothing was heard of it, save sotto voce, perhaps, at the Papal courts of the sixteenth century. To revive it publicly, or at least as much of it as could be borne by a world now for seventeen centuries Christian, was the glory of the eighteenth century The moral scheme of Theodorus has now nearly vanished among us, at least as a confessed creed; and, in spite of the authority of Mr. Locke's great and good name, his metaphysical scheme is showing signs of a like approaching disappearance. Let us hope that it may be a speedy one; for if the senses be the only avenues to knowledge; if man be the measure of all things; and if law have not, as Hooker says, her fount and home in the very bosom of God himself, then was Homer's Zeus right in declaring man to be "the most wretched of all the beasts of the field."

And yet one cannot help looking with a sort of awe (I dare not call it respect) at that melancholic faithless Hegesias. Doubtless he, like his compeers, and indeed all Alexandria for three hundred years, cultivated philosophy with no more real purpose than it was cultivated by the graceless beaux-esprits of Louis XV.'s court, and with as little practical effect on morality; but of this Hegesias alone it stands written, that his teaching actually made men do something, and moreover, do the most solemn and important thing which any man can do, excepting always doing right. I must confess, however, that the result of his teaching took so unexpected a form, that the reigning Ptolemy, apparently Philadelphus, had to interfere with the sacred right of every man to talk as much nonsense as he likes, and forbade Hegesias to teach at Alexandria. For Hegesias, a Cyrenaic like Theodorus, but a rather more morose pedant than that saucy and happy scoffer, having discovered that the great end of man was to avoid pain, also discovered (his digestion being probably in a disordered state) that there was so much more pain than pleasure in the world, as to make it a thoroughly disagreeable place, of which man was well rid at any price. Whereon he wrote a book called, [Greek text: apokarteroon], in which a man who had determined to starve himself, preached the miseries of human life, and the blessings of death, with such overpowering force, that the book actually drove many persons to commit suicide, and escape from a world which was not fit to dwell in. A fearful proof of how rotten the state of society was becoming, how desperate the minds of men, during those frightful centuries which immediately preceded the Christian era, and how fast was approaching that dark chaos of unbelief and unrighteousness, which Paul of Tarsus so analyses and describes in the first chapter of his Epistle to the Romans--when the old light was lost, the old faiths extinct, the old reverence for the laws of family and national life, destroyed, yea even the natural instincts themselves perverted; that chaos whose darkness Juvenal, and Petronius, and Tacitus have proved, in their fearful pages, not to have been exaggerated by the more compassionate though more righteous Jew.

And now observe, that this selfishness--this wholesome state of equilibrium--this philosophic calm, which is really only a lazy pride, was, as far as we can tell, the main object of all the schools from the time of Alexander to the Christian era. We know very little of those Sceptics, Cynics, Epicureans, Academics, Peripatetics, Stoics, of whom there has been so much talk, except at second-hand, through the Romans, from whom Stoicism in after ages received a new and not ignoble life. But this we do know of the later sets, that they gradually gave up the search for truth, and propounded to themselves as the great type for a philosopher, How shall a man save his own soul from this evil world? They may have been right; it may have been the best thing to think about in those exhausted and decaying times: but it was a question of ethics, not of philosophy, in the sense which the old Greek sages put on that latter word. Their object was, not to get at the laws of all things, but to fortify themselves against all things, each according to his scheme, and so to be self-sufficient and alone. Even in the Stoics, who boldly and righteously asserted an immutable morality, this was the leading conception. As has been well said of them:

"If we reflect how deeply the feeling of an intercourse between men and a divine race superior to themselves had worked itself into the Greek character--what a number of fables, some beautiful, some impure, it had impregnated and procured credence for--how it sustained every form of polity and every system of laws, we may imagine what the effects must have been of its disappearance. If it is possible for any man, it was not, certainly, possible for a Greek, to feel himself connected by any real bonds with his fellow-creatures around him, while he felt himself utterly separated from any being above his fellow-creatures. But the sense of that isolation would affect different minds very differently. It drove the Epicurean to consider how he might make a world in which he should live comfortably, without distracting visions of the past and future, and the dread of those upper powers who no longer awakened in him any feelings of sympathy. It drove Zeno the Stoic to consider whether a man may not find enough in himself to satisfy him, though what is beyond him be ever so unfriendly. . . . We may trace in the productions which are attributed to Zone a very clear indication of the feeling which was at work in his mind. He undertook, for instance, among other tasks, to answer Plato's 'Republic.' The truth that a man is a political being, which informs and pervades that book, was one which must have been particularly harassing to his mind, and which he felt must be got rid of, before he could hope to assert his doctrine of a man's solitary dignity."

Woe to the nation or the society in which this individualising and separating process is going on in the human mind! Whether it take the form of a religion or of a philosophy, it is at once the sign and the cause of senility, decay, and death. If man begins to forget that he is a social being, a member of a body, and that the only truths which can avail him anything, the only truths which are worthy objects of his philosophical search, are those which are equally true for every man, which will equally avail every man, which he must proclaim, as far as he can, to every man, from the proudest sage to the meanest outcast, he enters, I believe, into a lie, and helps forward the dissolution of that society of which he is a member. I care little whether what he holds be true or not. If it be true, he has made it a lie by appropriating it proudly and selfishly to himself, and by excluding others from it. He has darkened his own power of vision by that act of self-appropriation, so that even if he sees a truth, he can only see it refractedly, discoloured by the medium of his own private likes and dislikes, and fulfils that great and truly philosophic law, that he who loveth not his brother is in darkness, and knoweth not whither he goeth. And so it befell those old Greek schools. It is out of our path to follow them to Italy, where sturdy old Roman patriots cursed them, and with good reason, as corrupting the morals of the young. Our business is with Alexandria; and there, certainly, they did nothing for the elevation of humanity. What culture they may have given, probably helped to make the Alexandrians, what Caesar calls them, the most ingenious of all nations: but righteous or valiant men it did not make them. When, after the three great reigns of Soter, Philadelphus, and Euergetes, the race of the Ptolemies began to wear itself out, Alexandria fell morally, as its sovereigns fell; and during a miserable and shameful decline of a hundred and eighty years, sophists wrangled, pedants fought over accents and readings with the true odium gammaticum, and kings plunged deeper and deeper into the abysses of luxury and incest, laziness and cruelty, till the flood came, and swept them all away. Cleopatra, the Helen of Egypt, betrayed her country to the Roman; and thenceforth the Alexandrians became slaves in all but name.

And now that Alexandria has become a tributary province, is it to share the usual lot of enslaved countries and lose all originality and vigour of thought? Not so. From this point, strangely enough, it begins to have a philosophy of its own. Hitherto it has been importing Greek thought into Egypt and Syria, even to the furthest boundaries of Persia; and the whole East has become Greek: but it has received little in return. The Indian Gymnosophists, or Brahmins, had little or no effect on Greek philosophy, except in the case of Pyrrho: the Persian Dualism still less. The Egyptian symbolic nature-worship had been too gross to be regarded by the cultivated Alexandrian as anything but a barbaric superstition. One eastern nation had intermingled closely with the Macedonian race, and from it Alexandrian thought received a new impulse.

I mentioned in my first lecture the conciliatory policy which the Ptolemies had pursued toward the Jews. Soter had not only allowed but encouraged them to settle in Alexandria and Egypt, granting them the same political privileges with the

Macedonians and other Greeks. Soon they built themselves a temple there, in obedience to some supposed prophecy in their sacred writings, which seems most probably to have been a wilful interpolation. Whatsoever value we may attach to the various myths concerning the translation of their Scriptures into Greek, there can be no doubt that they were translated in the reign of Soter, and that the exceedingly valuable Septuagint version is the work of that period. Moreover, their numbers in Alexandria were very great. When Amrou took Constantinople in A.D. 640, there were 40,000 Jews in it; and their numbers during the Ptolemaic and Roman periods, before their temporary expulsion by Cyril about 412, were probably greater; and Egypt altogether is said to have contained 200,000 Jews. They had schools there, which were so esteemed by their whole nation throughout the East, that the Alexandrian Rabbis, the Light of Israel, as they were called, may be fairly considered as the centre of Jewish thought and learning for several centuries.

We are accustomed, and not without reason, to think with some contempt of these old Rabbis. Rabbinism, Cabbalism, are become by-words in the mouths of men. It may be instructive for us--it is certainly necessary for us, if we wish to understand Alexandria--to examine a little how they became so fallen.

Their philosophy took its stand, as you all know, on certain ancient books of their people; histories, laws, poems, philosophical treatises, which all have one element peculiar to themselves, namely, the assertion of a living personal Ruler and Teacher, not merely of the Jewish race, but of all the nations of the earth. After the return of their race from Babylon, their own records give abundant evidence that this strange people became the most exclusive and sectarian which the world ever saw. Into the causes of that exclusiveness I will not now enter; suffice it to say, that it was pardonable enough in a people asserting Monotheism in the midst of idolatrous nations, and who knew, from experience even more bitter than that which taught Plato and Socrates, how directly all those popular idolatries led to every form of baseness and immorality. But we may trace in them, from the date of their return from Babylon, especially from their settlement in Alexandria, a singular change of opinion. In proportion as they began to deny that their unseen personal Ruler had anything to do with the Gentiles--the nations of the earth, as they called them--in proportion as they considered themselves as His only subjects--or rather, Him and His guidance as their own private property--exactly in that proportion they began to lose all living or practical belief that He did guide them. He became a being of the past; one who had taught and governed their forefathers in old times: not one who was teaching and governing them now. I beg you to pay attention to this curious result; because you will see, I think, the very same thing occurring in two other Alexandrian schools, of which I shall speak hereafter.

The result to these Rabbis was, that the inspired books which spoke of this Divine guidance and government became objects of superstitious reverence, just in proportion as they lost all understanding of their real value and meaning. Nevertheless, this too produced good results; for the greatest possible care was taken to fix the Canon of these books; to settle, as far as possible, the exact time at which the Divine guidance was supposed to have ceased; after which it was impious to claim a Divine teaching; when their sages were left to themselves, as they fancied, with a complete body of knowledge, on which they were henceforth only to comment. Thus, whether or not they were right in supposing that the Divine Teacher had ceased to teach and inspire them, they did infinite service by marking out for us certain writers whom He had certainly taught and inspired. No doubt they were right in their sense of the awful change which had passed over their nation. There was an infinite difference between them and the old Hebrew writers. They had lost something which those old prophets possessed. I invite you to ponder, each for himself, on the causes of this strange loss; bearing in mind that they lost their forefathers' heirloom, exactly in proportion as they began to believe it to be their exclusive possession, and to deny other human beings any right to or share in it. It may have been that the light given to their forefathers had, as they thought, really departed. It may have been, also, that the light was there all around them still, as bright as ever, but that they would not open their eyes and behold it; or rather, could not open them, because selfishness and pride had sealed them. It may have been, that inspiration was still very near them too, if their spirits had been willing to receive it. But of the fact of the change there was no doubt. For the old Hebrew seers were men dealing with the loftiest and deepest laws: the Rabbis were shallow pedants. The old Hebrew seers were righteous and virtuous men: the Rabbis became, in due time, some of the worst and wickedest men who ever trod this earth.

Thus they too had their share in that downward career of pedantry which we have seen characterise the whole past Alexandrine age. They, like Zenodotus and

Aristarchus, were commentators, grammarians, sectarian disputers: they were not thinkers or actors. Their inspired books were to them no more the words of living human beings who had sought for the Absolute Wisdom, and found it after many sins and doubts and sorrows. The human writers became in their eyes the puppets and mouthpieces of some magical influence, not the disciples of a living and loving person. The book itself was, in their belief, not in any true sense inspired, but magically dictated--by what power they cared not to define. His character was unimportant to them, provided He had inspired no nation but their own. But, thought they, if the words were dictated, each of them must have some mysterious value. And if each word had a mysterious value, why not each letter? And how could they set limits to that mysterious value? Might not these words, even rearrangements of the letters of them, be useful in protecting them against the sorceries of the heathen, in driving away those evil spirits, or evoking those good spirits, who, though seldom mentioned in their early records, had after their return from Babylon begun to form an important part of their unseen world? For as they had lost faith in the One Preserver of their race, they had filled up the void by a ponderous demonology of innumerable preservers. This process of thought was not confined to Alexandria. Dr. Layard, in his last book on Nineveh, gives some curious instances of its prevalence among them at an earlier period, well worth your careful study. But it was at Alexandria that the Jewish Cabbalism formed itself into a system. It was there that the Jews learnt to become the jugglers and magic-mongers of the whole Roman world, till Claudius had to expel them from Rome, as pests to rational and moral society.

And yet, among these hapless pedants there lingered nobler thoughts and hopes. They could not read the glorious heirlooms of their race without finding in them records of antique greatness and virtue, of old deliverances worked for their forefathers; and what seemed promises, too, that that greatness should return. The notion that those promises were conditional; that they expressed eternal moral laws, and declared the consequences of obeying those laws, they had lost long ago. By looking on themselves as exclusively and arbitrarily favoured by Heaven, they were ruining their own moral sense. Things were not right or wrong to them because Right was eternal and divine, and Wrong the transgression of that eternal right. How could that be? For then the right things the Gentiles seemed to do would be right and divine;--and that supposition in their eyes was all but impious. None could do right but themselves, for they only knew the law of God. So, right with them had no absolute or universal ground, but was reduced in their minds to the performance of certain acts commanded exclusively to them--a form of ethics which rapidly sank into the most petty and frivolous casuistry as to the outward performance of those acts. The sequel of those ethics is known to all the world, in the spectacle of the most unrivalled religiosity, and scrupulous respectability, combined with a more utter absence of moral sense, in their most cultivated and learned men, than the world has ever beheld before or since.

In such a state of mind it was impossible for them to look on their old prophets as true seers, beholding and applying eternal moral laws, and, therefore, seeing the future in the present and in the past. They must be the mere utterers of an irreversible arbitrary fate; and that fate must, of course, be favourable to their nation. So now arose a school who picked out from their old prophets every passage which could be made to predict their future glory, and a science which settled when that glory was to return. By the arbitrary rules of criticism a prophetic day was defined to mean a year; a week, seven years. The most simple and human utterances were found to have recondite meanings relative to their future triumph over the heathens whom they cursed and hated. If any of you ever come across the popular Jewish interpretations of The Song of Solomon, you will there see the folly in which acute and learned men can indulge themselves when they have lost hold of the belief in anything really absolute and eternal and moral, and have made Fate, and Time, and Self, their real deities. But this dream of a future restoration was in no wise ennobled, as far as we can see, with any desire for a moral restoration. They believed that a person would appear some day or other to deliver them. Even they were happily preserved by their sacred books from the notion that deliverance was to be found for them, or for any man, in an abstraction or notion ending in -ation or -ality. In justice to them it must be said, that they were too wise to believe that personal qualities, such as power, will, love, righteousness, could reside in any but in a person, or be manifested except by a person. And among the earlier of them the belief may have been, that the ancient unseen Teacher of their race would be their deliverer: but as they lost the thought of Him, the expected Deliverer became a mere human being: or rather not a human being; for as they lost their moral sense, they lost in the very deepest meaning their humanity, and forgot what man was like till they learned to look only for a conqueror; a manifestation of power, and not of goodness; a destroyer of the hated heathen, who was to establish them as the tyrant race of the whole earth. On that fearful day on which, for a moment, they cast away even that last dream, and cried, "We have no king but Caesar," they spoke the secret of their hearts. It was a Caesar, a Jewish Caesar, for whom they had been longing for centuries. And if they could not have such a deliverer, they would have none: they would take up with the best embodiment of brute Titanic power which they could find, and crucify the embodiment of Righteousness and Love. Amid all the metaphysical schools of Alexandria, I know none so deeply instructive as that school of the Rabbis, "the glory of Israel."

But you will say: "This does not look like a school likely to regenerate Alexandrian thought." True: and yet it did regenerate it, both for good and for evil; for these men had among them and preserved faithfully enough for all practical purposes, the old literature of their race; a literature which I firmly believe, if I am to trust the experience of 1900 years, is destined to explain all other literatures; because it has firm hold of the one eternal root-idea which gives life, meaning, Divine sanction, to every germ or fragment of human truth which is in any of them. It did so, at least, in Alexandria for the Greek literature. About the Christian era, a cultivated Alexandrian Jew, a disciple of Plato and of Aristotle, did seem to himself to find in the sacred books of his nation that which agreed with the deepest discoveries of Greek philosophy; which explained and corroborated them. And his announcement of this fact, weak and defective as it was, had the most enormous and unexpected results. The father of New Platonism was Philo the Jew.

LECTURE III--NEOPLATONISM

We now approach the period in which Alexandria began to have a philosophy of its own--to be, indeed, the leader of human thought for several centuries.

I shall enter on this branch of my subject with some fear and trembling; not only on account of my own ignorance, but on account of the great difficulty of handling it without trenching on certain controversial subjects which are rightly and wisely forbidden here. For there was not one school of Metaphysic at Alexandria: there were two; which, during the whole period of their existence, were in internecine struggle with each other, and yet mutually borrowing from each other; the Heathen, namely, and the Christian. And you cannot contemplate, still less can you understand, the one without the other. Some of late years have become all but unaware of the existence of that Christian school; and the word Philosophy, on the authority of Gibbon, who, however excellent an authority for facts, knew nothing about Philosophy, and cared less, has been used exclusively to express heathen thought; a misnomer which in Alexandria would have astonished Plotinus or Hypatia as much as it would Clement or Origen. I do not say that there is, or ought to be, a Christian Metaphysic. I am speaking, as you know, merely as a historian, dealing with facts; and I say that there was one; as profound, as scientific, as severe, as that of the Pagan Neoplatonists; starting indeed, as I shall show hereafter, on many points from common ground with theirs. One can hardly doubt, I should fancy, that many parts of St. John's Gospel and Epistles, whatever view we may take of them, if they are to be called anything, are to be called metaphysic and philosophic. And one can no more doubt that before writing them he had studied Philo, and was expanding Philo's thought in the direction which seemed fit to him, than we can doubt it of the earlier Neoplatonists. The technical language is often identical; so are the primary ideas from which he starts, howsoever widely the conclusions may differ. If Plotinus considered himself an intellectual disciple of Plato, so did Origen and Clemens. And I must, as I said before, speak of both, or of neither. My only hope of escaping delicate ground lies in the curious fact, that rightly or wrongly, the form in which Christianity presented itself to the old Alexandrian thinkers was so utterly different from the popular conception of it in modern England, that one may very likely be able to tell what little one knows about it, almost without mentioning a single doctrine which now influences the religious world.

But far greater is my fear, that to a modern British auditory, trained in the school of Locke, much of ancient thought, heathen as well as Christian, may seem so utterly the product of the imagination, so utterly without any corresponding reality in the universe, as to look like mere unintelligible madness. Still, I must try; only entreating my hearers to consider, that how much soever we may honour Locke and his great Scotch followers, we are not bound to believe them either infallible, or altogether world-embracing; that there have been other methods than theirs of conceiving the Unseen; that the common ground from which both Christian and heathen Alexandrians start, is not merely a private vagary of their own, but one which has been accepted undoubtingly, under so many various forms, by so many different races, as to give something of an inductive probability that it is not a mere dream, but may be a right and true instinct of the human mind. I mean the belief that the things which we see--nature and all her phenomena-- are temporal, and born only to die; mere shadows of some unseen realities, from whom their laws and life are derived; while the eternal things which subsist without growth, decay, or change, the only real, only truly existing things, in short, are certain things which are not seen; inappreciable by sense, or understanding, or imagination, perceived only by the conscience and the reason. And that, again, the problem of philosophy, the highest good for man, that for the sake of which death were a gain, without which life is worthless, a drudgery, a degradation, a failure, and a ruin, is to discover what those unseen eternal things are, to know them, possess them, be in harmony with them, and thereby alone to rise to any real and solid power, or safety, or nobleness. It is a strange dream. But you will see that it is one which does not bear much upon "points of controversy," any more than on "Locke's philosophy;" nevertheless, when we find this same strange dream arising, apparently without intercommunion of thought, among the old Hindoos, among the Greeks, among the Jews; and lastly, when we see it springing again in the Middle Age, in the mind of the almost forgotten author of the "Deutsche Theologie," and so becoming the parent, not merely of Luther's deepest belief, or of the German mystic schools of the seventeenth and eighteenth centuries, but of the great German Philosophy itself as developed by Kant, and Fichte, and Schelling, and Hegel, we must at least confess it to be a popular delusion, if nothing better, vast enough and common enough to be worth a little patient investigation, wheresoever we may find it stirring the human mind.

But I have hope, still, that I may find sympathy and comprehension among some, at least, of my audience, as I proceed to examine the ancient realist schools of Alexandria, on account of their knowledge of the modern realist schools of Germany. For I cannot but see, that a revulsion is taking place in the thoughts of our nation upon metaphysic subjects, and that Scotland, as usual, is taking the lead therein. That most illustrious Scotchman, Mr. Thomas Carlyle, first vindicated the great German Realists from the vulgar misconceptions about them which were so common at the beginning of this century, and brought the minds of studious men to a more just appreciation of the philosophic severity, the moral grandeur, of such thinkers as Emmanuel Kant, and Gottlieb Fichte. To another Scotch gentleman, who, I believe, has honoured me by his presence here to-night, we owe most valuable translations of some of Fichte's works; to be followed, I trust, by more. And though, as a humble disciple of Bacon, I cannot but think that the method both of Kant and Fichte possesses somewhat of the same inherent defect as the method of the Neoplatonist school, yet I should be most unfair did I not express my deep obligations to them, and advise all those to study them carefully, who wish to gain a clear conception either of the old Alexandrian schools, or of those intellectual movements which are agitating the modern mind, and which will, I doubt not, issue in a clearer light, and in a nobler life, if not for us, yet still for our children's children for ever.

The name of Philo the Jew is now all but forgotten among us. He was laughed out of sight during the last century, as a dreamer and an allegorist, who tried eclectically to patch together Plato and Moses. The present age, however, is rapidly beginning to suspect that all who thought before the eighteenth century were not altogether either fools or impostors; old wisdom is obtaining a fairer hearing day by day, and is found not to be so contradictory to new wisdom as was supposed. We are beginning, too, to be more inclined to justify Providence, by believing that lies are by their very nature impotent and doomed to die; that everything which has had any great or permanent influence on the human mind, must have in it some germ of eternal truth; and setting ourselves to separate that germ of truth from the mistakes which may have distorted and overlaid it. Let us believe, or at least hope, the same for a few minutes, of Philo, and try to find out what was the secret of his power, what the secret of his weakness.

First: I cannot think that he had to treat his own sacred books unfairly, to make them agree with the root-idea of Socrates and Plato. Socrates and Plato acknowledged a Divine teacher of the human spirit; that was the ground of their philosophy. So did the literature of the Jews. Socrates and Plato, with all the Greek sages till the Sophistic era, held that the object of philosophy was the search after that which truly exists: that he who found that, found wisdom: Philo's books taught him the same truth: but they taught him also, that the search for wisdom was not merely the search for that which is, but for Him who is; not for a thing, but for a person. I do not mean that Plato and the elder Greeks had not that object also in view; for I have said already that Theology was with them the ultimate object of all metaphysic science: but I do think that they saw it infinitely less clearly than the old Jewish sages. Those sages were utterly unable to conceive of an absolute truth, except as residing in an absolutely true person; of absolute wisdom, except in an absolutely wise person; of an absolute order and law, except in a lawgiver; of an absolute good, except in an absolutely good person: any more than either they or we can conceive of an absolute love, except in an absolutely loving person. I say boldly, that I think them right, on all grounds of Baconian induction. For all these qualities are only known to us as exhibited in persons; and if we believe them to have any absolute and eternal existence at all, to be objective, and independent of us, and the momentary moods and sentiments of our own mind, they must exist in some absolute and eternal person, or they are mere notions, abstractions, words, which have no counterparts.

But here arose a puzzle in the mind of Philo, as it in reality had, we may see, in the minds of Socrates and Plato. How could he reconcile the idea of that absolute and eternal one Being, that Zeus, Father of Gods and men, self-perfect, self-contained, without change or motion, in whom, as a Jew, he believed even more firmly than the Platonists, with the Daemon of Socrates, the Divine Teacher whom both Plato and Solomon confessed? Or how, again, could he reconcile the idea of Him with the creative and providential energy, working in space and time, working on matter, and apparently affected and limited, if not baffled, by the imperfection of the minds which he taught, by the imperfection of the matter which he moulded? This, as all students of philosophy must know, was one of the great puzzles of old Greek philosophy, as long as it was earnest and cared to have any puzzles at all: it has been, since the days of Spinoza, the great puzzle of all earnest modern philosophers. Philo offered a solution in that idea of a Logos, or Word of God, Divinity articulate, speaking and acting in time and space, and therefore by successive acts; and so doing, in time and space, the will of the timeless and spaceless Father, the Abysmal and Eternal Being, of whom he was the perfect likeness. In calling this person the Logos, and making him the source of all human reason, and knowledge of eternal laws, he only translated from Hebrew into Greek the name which he found in his sacred books, "The Word of God." As yet we have found no unfair allegorising of Moses, or twisting of Plato. How then has he incurred this accusation?

I cannot think, again, that he was unfair in supposing that he might hold at the same time the Jewish belief concerning Creation, and the Platonic doctrine of the real existence of Archetypal ideas, both of moral and of physical phenomena. I do not mean that such a conception was present consciously to the mind of the old Jews, as it was most certainly to the mind of St. Paul, a practised Platonic dialectician; but it seems to me, as to Philo, to be a fair, perhaps a necessary, corollary from the Genetic Philosophy, both of Moses and of Solomon.

But in one thing he was unfair; namely, in his allegorising. But unfair to whom? To Socrates and Plato, I believe, as much as to Moses and to Samuel. For what is the part of the old Jewish books which he evaporates away into mere mystic symbols of the private experiences of the devout philosopher? Its practical everyday histories, which deal with the common human facts of family and national life, of man's outward and physical labour and craft. These to him have no meaning, except an allegoric one. But has he thrown them away for the sake of getting a step nearer to Socrates, or Plato, or Aristotle? Surely not. To them, as to the old Jewish sages, man is most important when regarded not merely as a soul, but as a man, a social being of flesh and blood. Aristotle declares politics to be the architectonical science, the family and social relations to be the eternal master-facts of humanity. Plato, in his Republic, sets before himself the Constitution of a State, as the crowning problem of his philosophy. Every work of his, like every saying of his master Socrates, deals with the common, outward, vulgar facts of human life, and asserts that there is a divine meaning in them, and that reverent induction from them is the way to obtain the deepest truths. Socrates and Plato were as little inclined to separate the man and the philosopher as Moses, Solomon, or Isaiah were. When Philo, by allegorising away the simple human parts of his books, is untrue to Moses's teaching, he becomes untrue to Plato's. He becomes untrue, I believe, to a higher teaching than Plato's. He loses sight of an eternal truth, which even old Homer might have taught him, when he treats Moses as one section of his disciples in after years treated Homer.

For what is the secret of the eternal freshness, the eternal beauty, ay, I may say

boldly, in spite of all their absurdities and immoralities, the eternal righteousness
of those old Greek myths? What is it which made Socrates and Plato cling lovingly
and reverently to them, they scarce knew why, while they deplored the immoralities to which they had given rise? What is it which made those myths, alone of all
old mythologies, the parents of truly beautiful sculpture, painting, poetry? What is
it which makes us love them still; find, even at times against our consciences, new
meaning, new beauty in them; and brings home the story of Perseas or of Hercules,
alike to the practised reason of Niebuhr, and the untutored instincts of Niebuhr's
little child, for whom he threw them into simplest forms? Why is it that in spite of
our disagreeing with their creed and their morality, we still persist--and long may
we persist, or rather be compelled--as it were by blind instinct, to train our boys
upon those old Greek dreams; and confess, whenever we try to find a substitute
for them in our educational schemes, that we have as yet none? Because those old
Greek stories do represent the Deities as the archetypes, the kinsmen, the teachers, the friends, the inspirers of men. Because while the schoolboy reads how the
Gods were like to men, only better, wiser, greater; how the Heroes are the children
of the Gods, and the slayers of the monsters which devour the earth; how Athene
taught men weaving, and Phoebus music, and Vulcan the cunning of the stithy;
how the Gods took pity on the noble- hearted son of Danae, and lent him celestial
arms and guided him over desert and ocean to fulfil his vow--that boy is learning
deep lessons of metaphysic, more in accordance with the reine vernunft, the pure
reason whereby man perceives that which is moral, and spiritual, and eternal, than
he would from all disquisitions about being and becoming, about actualities and
potentialities, which ever tormented the weary brain of man.

Let us not despise the gem because it has been broken to fragments, obscured
by silt and mud. Still less let us fancy that one least fragment of it is not more precious than the most brilliant paste jewel of our own compounding, though it be polished and faceted never so completely. For what are all these myths but fragments
of that great metaphysic idea, which, I boldly say, I believe to be at once the justifier
and the harmoniser of all philosophic truth which man has ever discovered, or will
discover; which Philo saw partially, and yet clearly; which the Hebrew sages perceived far more deeply, because more humanly and practically; which Saint Paul
the Platonist, and yet the Apostle, raised to its highest power, when he declared

that the immutable and self-existent Being, for whom the Greek sages sought, and did not altogether seek in vain, has gathered together all things both in heaven and in earth in one inspiring and creating Logos, who is both God and Man?

Be this as it may, we find that from the time of Philo, the deepest thought of the heathen world began to flow in a theologic channel. All the great heathen thinkers henceforth are theologians. In the times of Nero, for instance, Epictetus the slave, the regenerator of Stoicism, is no mere speculator concerning entities and quiddities, correct or incorrect. He is a slave searching for the secret of freedom, and finding that it consists in escaping not from a master, but from self: not to wealth and power, but to Jove. He discovers that Jove is, in some most mysterious, but most real sense, the Father of men; he learns to look up to that Father as his guide and friend.

Numenius, again, in the second century, was a man who had evidently studied Philo. He perceived so deeply, I may say so exaggeratedly, the analogy between the Jewish and the Platonic assertions of an Absolute and Eternal Being, side by side with the assertion of a Divine Teacher of man, that he is said to have uttered the startling saying: "What is Plato but Moses talking Attic?" Doubtless Plato is not that: but the expression is remarkable, as showing the tendency of the age. He too looks up to God with prayers for the guidance of his reason. He too enters into speculation concerning God in His absoluteness, and in His connection with the universe. "The Primary God," he says, "must be free from works and a King; but the Demiurgus must exercise government, going through the heavens. Through Him comes this our condition; through Him Reason being sent down in efflux, holds communion with all who are prepared for it: God then looking down, and turning Himself to each of us, it comes to pass that our bodies live and are nourished, receiving strength from the outer rays which come from Him. But when God turns us to the contemplation of Himself, it comes to pass that these things are worn out and consumed, but that the reason lives, being partaker of a blessed life."

This passage is exceedingly interesting, as containing both the marrow of old Hebrew metaphysic, and also certain notional elements, of which we find no trace in the Scripture, and which may lead--as we shall find they afterwards did lead--to confusing the moral with the notional, and finally the notional with the material; in plain words, to Pantheism.

You find this tendency, in short, in all the philosophers who flourished between the age of Augustus and the rise of Alexandrian Neoplatonism. Gibbon, while he gives an approving pat on the back to his pet "Philosophic Emperor," Marcus Aurelius, blinks the fact that Marcus's philosophy, like that of Plutarch, contains as an integral element, a belief which to him would have been, I fear, simply ludicrous, from its strange analogy with the belief of John, the Christian Apostle. What is Marcus Aurelius's cardinal doctrine? That there is a God within him, a Word, a Logos, which "has hold of him," and who is his teacher and guardian; that over and above his body and his soul, he has a Reason which is capable of "hearing that Divine Word, and obeying the monitions of that God." What is Plutarch's cardinal doctrine? That the same Word, the Daemon who spoke to the heart of Socrates, is speaking to him and to every philosopher; "coming into contact," he says, "with him in some wonderful manner; addressing the reason of those who, like Socrates, keep their reason pure, not under the dominion of passion, nor mixing itself greatly with the body, and therefore quick and sensitive in responding to that which encountered it.

You see from these two extracts what questions were arising in the minds of men, and how they touched on ethical and theological questions. I say arising in their minds: I believe that I ought to say rather, stirred up in their minds by One greater than they. At all events, there they appeared, utterly independent of any Christian teaching. The belief in this Logos or Daemon speaking to the Reason of man, was one which neither Plutarch nor Marcus, neither Numenius nor Ammonius, as far as we can see, learnt from the Christians; it was the common ground which they held with them; the common battlefield which they disputed with them.

Neither have we any reason to suppose that they learnt it from the Hindoos. That much Hindoo thought mixed with Neoplatonist speculation we cannot doubt; but there is not a jot more evidence to prove that Alexandrians borrowed this conception from the Mahabharavata, than that George Fox the Quaker, or the author of the "Deutsche Theologie," did so. They may have gone to Hindoo philosophy, or rather, to second and third hand traditions thereof, for corroborations of the belief; but be sure, it must have existed in their own hearts first, or they would never have gone thither. Believe it; be sure of it. No earnest thinker is a plagiarist pure and simple. He will never borrow from others that which he has not already, more or less, thought out for himself. When once a great idea, instinctive, inductive (for the two expressions are nearer akin than most fancy), has dawned on his soul, he will welcome lovingly, awfully, any corroboration from foreign schools, and cry with joy: "Behold, this is not altogether a dream: for others have found it also. Surely it must be real, universal, eternal." No; be sure there is far more originality (in the common sense of the word), and far less (in the true sense of the word), than we fancy; and that it is a paltry and shallow doctrine which represents each succeeding school as merely the puppets and dupes of the preceding. More originality, because each earnest man seems to think out for himself the deepest grounds of his creed. Less originality, because, as I believe, one common Logos, Word, Reason, reveals and unveils the same eternal truth to all who seek and hunger for it.

Therefore we can, as the Christian philosophers of Alexandria did, rejoice over every truth which their heathen adversaries beheld, and attribute them, as Clement does, to the highest source, to the inspiration of the one and universal Logos. With Clement, philosophy is only hurtful when it is untrue to itself, and philosophy falsely so called; true philosophy is an image of the truth, a divine gift bestowed on the Greeks. The Bible, in his eyes, asserts that all forms of art and wisdom are from God. The wise in mind have no doubt some peculiar endowment of nature, but when they have offered themselves for their work, they receive a spirit of perception from the Highest Wisdom, giving them a new fitness for it. All severe study, all cultivation of sympathy, are exercises of this spiritual endowment. The whole intellectual discipline of the Greeks, with their philosophy, came down from God to men. Philosophy, he concludes in one place, carries on "an inquiry concerning Truth and the nature of Being; and this Truth is that concerning which the Lord Himself said: 'I am the Truth.' And when the initiated find, or rather receive, the true philosophy, they have it from the Truth itself; that is from Him who is true."

While, then, these two schools had so many grounds in common, where was their point of divergence? We shall find it, I believe, fairly expressed in the dying words of Plotinus, the great father of Neoplatonism. "I am striving to bring the God which is in us into harmony with the God which is in the universe." Whether or not Plotinus actually so spoke, that was what his disciples not only said that he spoke, but what they would have wished him to speak. That one sentence expresses the whole object of their philosophy.

But to that Pantaenus, Origen, Clement, and Augustine would have answered: "And we, on the other hand, assert that the God which is in the universe, is the same as the God which is in you, and is striving to bring you into harmony with Himself." There is the experimentum crucis. There is the vast gulf between the Christian and the Heathen schools, which when any man had overleaped, the whole problem of the universe was from that moment inverted. With Plotinus and his school man is seeking for God: with Clement and his, God is seeking for man. With the former, God is passive, and man active: with the latter, God is active, man is passive--passive, that is, in so far as his business is to listen when he is spoken to, to look at the light which is unveiled to him, to submit himself to the inward laws which he feels reproving and checking him at every turn, as Socrates was reproved and checked by his inward Daemon.

Whether of these two theorems gives the higher conception either of the Divine Being, or of man, I leave it for you to judge. To those old Alexandrian Christians, a being who was not seeking after every single creature, and trying to raise him, could not be a Being of absolute Righteousness, Power, Love; could not be a Being worthy of respect or admiration, even of philosophic speculation. Human righteousness and love flows forth disinterestedly to all around it, however unconscious, however unworthy they may be; human power associated with goodness, seeks for objects which it may raise and benefit by that power. We must confess this, with the Christian schools, or, with the Heathen schools, we must allow another theory, which brought them into awful depths; which may bring any generation which holds it into the same depths.

If Clement had asked the Neoplatonists: "You believe, Plotinus, in an absolutely Good Being. Do you believe that it desires to shed forth its goodness on all?" "Of course," they would have answered, "on those who seek for it, on the philosopher."

"But not, it seems, Plotinus, on the herd, the brutal, ignorant mass, wallowing in those foul crimes above which you have risen?" And at that question there would have been not a little hesitation. These brutes in human form, these souls wallowing in earthly mire, could hardly, in the Neoplatonists' eyes, be objects of the Divine desire.

"Then this Absolute Good, you say, Plotinus, has no relation with them, no care to raise them. In fact, it cannot raise them, because they have nothing in common with it. Is that your notion?" And the Neoplatonists would have, on the whole, allowed that argument. And if Clement had answered, that such was not his notion of Goodness, or of a Good Being, and that therefore the goodness of their Absolute Good, careless of the degradation and misery around it, must be something very different from his notions of human goodness; the Neoplatonists would have answered-- indeed they did answer--"After all, why not? Why should the Absolute Goodness be like our human goodness?" This is Plotinus's own belief. It is a question with him, it was still more a question with those who came after him, whether virtues could be predicated of the Divine nature; courage, for instance, of one who had nothing to fear; self- restraint, of one who had nothing to desire. And thus, by setting up a different standard of morality for the divine and for the human, Plotinus gradually arrives at the conclusion, that virtue is not the end, but the means; not the Divine nature itself, as the Christian schools held, but only the purgative process by which man was to ascend into heaven, and which was necessary to arrive at that nature--that nature itself being--what?

And how to answer that last question was the abysmal problem of the whole of Neoplatonic philosophy, in searching for which it wearied itself out, generation after generation, till tired equally of seeking and of speaking, it fairly lay down and died. In proportion as it refused to acknowledge a common divine nature with the degraded mass, it deserted its first healthy instinct, which told it that the spiritual world is identical with the moral world, with right, love, justice; it tried to find new definitions for the spiritual; it conceived it to be identical with the intellectual. That did not satisfy its heart. It had to repeople the spiritual world, which it had emptied of its proper denizens, with ghosts; to reinvent the old daemonologies and polytheisms--from thence to descend into lower depths, of which we will speak hereafter.

But in the meanwhile we must look at another quarrel which arose between the two twin schools of Alexandria. The Neoplatonists said that there is a divine element in man. The Christian philosophers assented fervently, and raised the old disagreeable question: "Is it in every man? In the publicans and harlots as well as in the philosophers? We say that it is." And there again the Neoplatonist finds it over hard to assent to a doctrine, equally contrary to outward appearance, and galling to Pharisaic pride; and enters into a hundred honest self- puzzles and self-contradictions, which seem to justify him at last in saying, No. It is in the philosopher, who is ready by nature, as Plotinus has it, and as it were furnished with wings, and not needing to sever himself from matter like the rest, but disposed already to ascend to that which is above. And in a degree too, it is in the "lover," who, according to Plotinus, has a certain innate recollection of beauty, and hovers round it, and desires it, wherever he sees it. Him you may raise to the apprehension of the one incorporeal Beauty, by teaching him to separate beauty from the various objects in which it appears scattered and divided. And it is even in the third class, the lowest of whom there is hope, namely, the musical man, capable of being passively affected by beauty, without having any active appetite for it; the sentimentalist, in short, as we should call him nowadays.

But for the herd, Plotinus cannot say that there is anything divine in them. And thus it gradually comes out in all Neoplatonist writings which I have yet examined, that the Divine only exists in a man, in proportion as he is conscious of its existence in him. From which spring two conceptions of the Divine in man. First, is it a part of him, if it is dependent for its existence on his consciousness of it? Or is it, as Philo, Plutarch, Marcus Aurelius would have held, as the Christians held, something independent of him, without him, a Logos or Word speaking to his reason and conscience? With this question Plotinus grapples, earnestly, shrewdly, fairly. If you wish to see how he does it, you should read the fourth and fifth books of the sixth Ennead, especially if you be lucky enough to light on a copy of that rare book, Taylor's faithful though crabbed translation.

Not that the result of his search is altogether satisfactory. He enters into subtle and severe disquisitions concerning soul. Whether it is one or many. How it can be both one and many. He has the strongest perception that, to use the noble saying of the Germans, "Time and Space are no gods." He sees clearly that the soul, and the whole unseen world of truly existing being, is independent of time and space: and yet, after he has wrestled with the two Titans, through page after page, and apparently conquered them, they slip in again unawares into the battle- field, the moment his back is turned. He denies that the one Reason has parts--it must exist as a whole wheresoever it exists: and yet he cannot express the relation of the individual soul to it, but by saying that we are parts of it; or that each thing, down to the lowest, receives as much soul as it is capable of possessing. Ritter has worked out at length, though in a somewhat dry and lifeless way, the hundred contradictions of this kind which you meet in Plotinus; contradictions which I suspect to be inseparable from any philosophy starting from his grounds. Is he not looking for the spiritual in a region where it does not exist; in the region of logical conceptions and abstractions, which are not realities, but only, after all, symbols of our own, whereby we express to ourselves the processes of our own brain? May not his Christian contemporaries have been nearer scientific truth, as well as nearer the common sense and practical belief of mankind, in holding that that which is spiritual is personal, and can only be seen or conceived of as residing in persons; and that that which is personal is moral, and has to do, not with abstractions of the intellect, but with right and wrong, love and hate, and all which, in the common instincts of men, involves a free will, a free judgment, a free responsibility and desert? And that, therefore, if there were a Spirit, a Daemonic Element, an universal Reason, a Logos, a Divine Element, closely connected with man, that one Reason, that one Divine Element, must be a person also? At least, so strong was the instinct of even the Heathen schools in this direction, that the followers of Plotinus had to fill up the void which yawned between man and the invisible things after which he yearned, by reviving the whole old Pagan Polytheism, and adding to it a Daemonology borrowed partly from the Chaldees, and partly from the Jewish rabbis, which formed a descending chain of persons, downward from the highest Deities to heroes, and to the guardian angel of each man; the meed of the philosopher being, that by self-culture and self-restraint he could rise above the tutelage of some lower and more earthly daemon, and become the pupil of a God, and finally a God himself.

These contradictions need not lower the great Father of Neoplatonism in our eyes, as a moral being. All accounts of him seem to prove him to have been what Apollo, in a lengthy oracle, declared him to have been, "good and gentle, and benignant exceedingly, and pleasant in all his conversation." He gave good advice about earthly matters, was a faithful steward of moneys deposited with him, a guardian of widows and orphans, a righteous and loving man. In his practical life, the ascetic and gnostic element comes out strongly enough. The body, with him, was not evil, neither was it good; it was simply nothing--why care about it? He would have no portrait taken of his person: "It was humiliating enough to be obliged to carry a shadow about with him, without having a shadow made of that shadow." He refused animal food, abstained from baths, declined medicine in his last illness, and so died about 200 A.D.

It is in his followers, as one generally sees in such cases, that the weakness of his conceptions comes out. Plotinus was an earnest thinker, slavishly enough reverencing the opinion of Plato, whom he quotes as an infallible oracle, with a "He says," as if there were but one he in the universe: but he tried honestly to develop Plato, or what he conceived to be Plato, on the method which Plato had laid down. His dialectic is far superior, both in quantity and in quality, to that of those who come after him. He is a seeker. His followers are not. The great work which marks the second stage of his school is not an inquiry, but a justification, not only of the Egyptian, but of all possible theurgies and superstitions; perhaps the best attempt of the kind which the world has ever seen; that which marks the third is a mere cloud-castle, an inverted pyramid, not of speculation, but of dogmatic assertion, patched together from all accessible rags and bones of the dead world. Some here will, perhaps, guess from my rough descriptions, that I speak of Iamblichus and Proclus.

Whether or not Iamblichus wrote the famous work usually attributed to him, which describes itself as the letter of Abamnon the Teacher to Porphyry, he became the head of that school of Neoplatonists who fell back on theurgy and magic, and utterly swallowed up the more rational, though more hopeless, school of Porphyry. Not that Porphyry, too, with all his dislike of magic and the vulgar superstitions--a dislike intimately connected with his loudly expressed dislike of the common herd, and therefore of Christianity, as a religion for the common herd-- did not believe a fact or two, which looks to us, nowadays, somewhat unphilosophical. From him we learn that one Ammonius, trying to crush Plotinus by magic arts, had his weapons so completely turned against himself, that all his limbs were contracted. From him we learn that Plotinus, having summoned in the temple of Isis his familiar spirit, a god, and not a mere daemon, appeared. He writes sensibly enough however to one Anebos, an Egyptian priest, stating his doubts as to the popular notions of the Gods, as beings subject to human passions and vices, and of theurgy and magic, as material means of compelling them to appear, or alluring them to favour man. The answer of Abamnon, Anebos, Iamblichus, or whoever the real author may have been, is worthy of perusal by every metaphysical student, as a curious phase of thought, not confined to that time, but rife, under some shape or other, in every age of the world's history, and in this as much as in any. There are many passages full of eloquence, many more full of true and noble thought: but on the whole, it is the sewing of new cloth into an old garment; the attempt to suit the old superstition to the new one, by eclectically picking and choosing, and special pleading, on both sides; but the rent is only made worse. There is no base superstition which Abamnon does not unconsciously justify. And yet he is rapidly losing sight of the real eternal human germs of truth round which those superstitions clustered, and is really further from truth and reason than old Homer or Hesiod, because further from the simple, universal, everyday facts, and relations, and duties of man, which are, after all, among the most mysterious, and also among the most sacred objects which man can contemplate.

It was not wonderful, however, that Neoplatonism took the course it did. Spirit, they felt rightly, was meant to rule matter; it was to be freed from matter only for that very purpose. No one could well deny that. The philosopher, as he rose and became, according to Plotinus, a god, or at least approached toward the gods, must partake of some mysterious and transcendental power. No one could well deny that conclusion, granting the premiss. But of what power? What had he to show as the result of his intimate communion with an unseen Being? The Christian Schools, who held that the spiritual is the moral, answered accordingly. He must show righteousness, and love, and peace in a Holy Spirit. That is the likeness of God. In proportion as a man has them, he is partaker of a Divine nature. He can rise no higher, and he needs no more. Platonists had said--No, that is only virtue; and virtue is the means, not the end. We want proof of having something above that; something more than any man of the herd, any Christian slave, can perform; something above nature; portents and wonders. So they set to work to perform wonders; and succeeded, I suppose, more or less. For now one enters into a whole fairyland of those very phenomena which are puzzling us so nowadays-- ecstasy, clairvoyance, insensibility to pain, cures produced by the effect of what we now call mesmerism. They are all there, these modern puzzles, in those old books of the long bygone seekers for wisdom. It makes us love them, while it saddens us to see that their difficulties were the same as ours, and that there is nothing new under the sun. Of course, a great deal of it all was "imagination." But the question then, as now is, what is this wonder-working imagination?--unless the word be used as a mere euphemism for lying, which really, in many cases, is hardly fair. We cannot wonder at the old Neoplatonists for attributing these strange phenomena to spiritual influence, when we see some who ought to know better doing the same thing now; and others, who more wisely believe them to be strictly physical and nervous, so utterly unable to give reasons for them, that they feel it expedient to ignore them for awhile, till they know more about those physical phenomena which can be put under some sort of classification, and attributed to some sort of inductive law.

But again. These ecstasies, cures, and so forth, brought them rapidly back to the old priestcrafts. The Egyptian priests, the Babylonian and Jewish sorcerers, had practised all this as a trade for ages, and reduced it to an art. It was by sleeping in the temples of the deities, after due mesmeric manipulations, that cures were even then effected. Surely the old priests were the people to whom to go for information. The old philosophers of Greece were venerable. How much more those of the East, in comparison with whom the Greeks were children? Besides, if these daemons and deities were so near them, might it not be possible to behold them? They seemed to have given up caring much for the world and its course -

Effugerant adytis templisque relictis Di quibus imperium steterat.

The old priests used to make them appear--perhaps they might do it again. And if spirit could act directly and preternaturally on matter, in spite of the laws of matter, perhaps matter might act on spirit. After all, were matter and spirit so absolutely different? Was not spirit some sort of pervading essence, some subtle ethereal fluid, differing from matter principally in being less gross and dense? This was the point to which they went down rapidly enough; the point to which all philosophies, I firmly believe, will descend, which do not keep in sight that the spiritual means the moral. In trying to make it mean exclusively the intellectual, they will degrade it to mean the merely logical and abstract; and when that is found to be a barren and lifeless phantom, a mere projection of the human brain, attributing reality to mere conceptions and names, and confusing the subject with the object, as logicians say truly the Neoplatonists did, then in despair, the school will try to make the spiritual something real, or, at least, something conceivable, by reinvesting it with the properties of matter, and talking of it as if it were some manner of gas, or heat, or electricity, or force, pervading time and space, conditioned by the accidents of brute matter, and a part of that nature which is born to die.

The culmination of all this confusion we see in Proclus. The unfortunate Hypatia, who is the most important personage between him and Iamblichus, has left no writings to our times; we can only judge of her doctrine by that of her instructors and her pupils. Proclus was taught by the men who had heard her lecture; and the golden chain of the Platonic succession descended from her to him. His throne, however, was at Athens, not at Alexandria. After the murder of the maiden philosopher, Neoplatonism prudently retired to Greece. But Proclus is so essentially the child of the Alexandrian school that we cannot pass him over. Indeed, according to M. Cousin, as I am credibly informed, he is the Greek philosopher; the flower and crown of all its schools; in whom, says the learned Frenchman, "are combined, and from whom shine forth, in no irregular or uncertain rays, Orpheus, Pythagoras, Plato, Aristotle, Zeno, Plotinus, Porphyry, and Iamblichus;" and who "had so comprehended all religions in his mind, and paid them such equal reverence, that he was, as it were, the priest of the whole universe!"

I have not the honour of knowing much of M. Cousin's works. I never came across them but on one small matter of fact, and on that I found him copying at second hand an anachronism which one would have conceived palpable to any reader of the original authorities. This is all I know of him, saving these his raptures over Proclus, of which I have quoted only a small portion, and of which I can only say, in Mr. Thomas Carlyle's words, "What things men will worship, in their extreme need!" Other moderns, however, have expressed their admiration of Proclus; and, no doubt, many neat sayings may be found in him (for after all he was a Greek), which will be both pleasing and useful to those who consider philosophic method to consist in putting forth strings of brilliant apophthegms, careless about either their consistency or coherence: but of the method of Plato or Aristotle, any more than of that of Kant or Mill, you will find nothing in him. He seems to my simplicity to be at once the most timid and servile of commentators, and the most cloudy of declaimers. He can rave symbolism like Jacob Bohmen, but without an atom of his originality and earnestness. He can develop an inverted pyramid of daemonology, like Father Newman himself, but without an atom of his art, his knowledge of human cravings. He combines all schools, truly, Chaldee and Egyptian as well as

Greek; but only scraps from their mummies, drops from their quintessences, which satisfy the heart and conscience as little as they do the logical faculties. His Greek gods and heroes, even his Alcibiades and Socrates, are "ideas;" that is, symbols of certain notions or qualities: their flesh and bones, their heart and brain, have been distilled away, till nothing is left but a word, a notion, which may patch a hole in his huge heaven-and-earth- embracing system. He, too, is a commentator and a deducer; all has been discovered; and he tries to discover nothing more. Those who followed him seem to have commented on his comments. With him Neoplatonism properly ends. Is its last utterance a culmination or a fall? Have the Titans sealed heaven, or died of old age, "exhibiting," as Gibbon says of them, "a deplorable instance of the senility of the human mind?" Read Proclus, and judge for yourselves: but first contrive to finish everything else you have to do which can possibly be useful to any human being. Life is short, and Art--at least the art of obtaining practical guidance from the last of the Alexandrians--very long.

And yet--if Proclus and his school became gradually unfaithful to the great root-idea of their philosophy, we must not imitate them. We must not believe that the last of the Alexandrians was under no divine teaching, because he had be-systemed himself into confused notions of what that teaching was like. Yes, there was good in poor old Proclus; and it too came from the only source whence all good comes. Were there no good in him I could not laugh at him as I have done; I could only hate him. There are moments when he rises above his theories; moments when he recurs in spirit, if not in the letter, to the faith of Homer, almost to the faith of Philo. Whether these are the passages of his which his modern admirers prize most, I cannot tell. I should fancy not: nevertheless I will read you one of them.

He is about to commence his discourses on the Parmenides, that book in which we generally now consider that Plato has been most untrue to himself, and fallen from his usual inductive method to the ground of a mere e priori theoriser--and yet of which Proclus is reported to have said, and, I should conceive, said honestly, that if it, the Timaeus, and the Orphic fragments were preserved, he did not care whether every other book on earth were destroyed. But how does he commence?

"I pray to all the gods and goddesses to guide my reason in the speculation which lies before me, and having kindled in me the pure light of truth, to direct my mind upward to the very knowledge of the things which are, and to open the doors of my soul to receive the divine guidance of Plato, and, having directed my knowledge into the very brightness of being, to withdraw me from the various forms of opinion, from the apparent wisdom, from the wandering about things which do not exist, by that purest intellectual exercise about the things which do exist, whereby alone the eye of the soul is nourished and brightened, as Socrates says in the Phaedrus; and that the Noetic Gods will give to me the perfect reason, and the Noeric Gods the power which leads up to this, and that the rulers of the Universe above the heaven will impart to me an energy unshaken by material notions and emancipated from them, and those to whom the world is given as their dominion a winged life, and the angelic choirs a true manifestation of divine things, and the good daemons the fulness of the inspiration which comes from the Gods, and the heroes a grand, and venerable, and lofty fixedness of mind, and the whole divine race together a perfect preparation for sharing in Plato's most mystical and far-seeing speculations, which he declares to us himself in the Parmenides, with the profundity befitting such topics, but which he (i.e. his master Syrianus) completed by his most pure and luminous apprehensions, who did most truly share the Platonic feast, and was the medium for transmitting the divine truth, the guide in our speculations, and the hierophant of these divine words; who, as I think, came down as a type of philosophy, to do good to the souls that are here, in place of idols, sacrifices, and the whole mystery of purification, a leader of salvation to the men who are now and who shall be hereafter. And may the whole band of those who are above us be propitious; and may the whole force which they supply be at hand, kindling before us that light which, proceeding from them, may guide us to them."

Surely this is an interesting document. The last Pagan Greek prayer, I believe, which we have on record; the death-wail of the old world--not without a touch of melody. One cannot altogether admire the style; it is inflated, pedantic, written, I fear, with a considerable consciousness that he was saying the right thing and in the very finest way: but still it is a prayer. A cry for light--by no means, certainly, like that noble one in Tennyson's "In Memoriam:"

So runs my dream. But what am I? An infant crying in the night; An infant crying for the light; And with no language but a cry.

Yet he asks for light: perhaps he had settled already for himself--like too many more of us--what sort of light he chose to have: but still the eye is turned upward to the sun, not inward in conceited fancy that self is its own illumination. He asks--surely not in vain. There was light to be had for asking. That prayer certainly was not answered in the letter: it may have been ere now in the spirit. And yet it is a sad prayer enough. Poor old man, and poor old philosophy!

This he and his teachers had gained by despising the simpler and yet far profounder doctrine of the Christian schools, that the Logos, the Divine Teacher in whom both Christians and Heathens believed, was the very archetype of men, and that He had proved that fact by being made flesh, and dwelling bodily among them, that they might behold His glory, full of grace and truth, and see that it was at once the perfection of man and the perfection of God: that that which was most divine was most human, and that which was most human, most divine. That was the outcome of their metaphysic, that they had found the Absolute One; because One existed in whom the apparent antagonism between that which is eternally and that which becomes in time, between the ideal and the actual, between the spiritual and the material, in a word, between God and man, was explained and reconciled for ever.

And Proclus's prayer, on the other hand, was the outcome of the Neoplatonists' metaphysic, the end of all their search after the One, the Indivisible, the Absolute, this cry to all manner of innumerable phantoms, ghosts of ideas, ghosts of traditions, neither things nor persons, but thoughts, to give the philosopher each something or other, according to the nature of each. Not that he very clearly defines what each is to give him; but still he feels himself in want of all manner of things, and it is as well to have as many friends at court as possible-- Noetic Gods, Noeric Gods, rulers, angels, daemons, heroes--to enable him to do what? To understand Plato's most mystical and far-seeing speculations. The Eternal Nous, the Intellectual Teacher has vanished further and further off; further off still some dim vision of a supreme Goodness. Infinite spaces above that looms through the mist of the abyss a Primaeval One. But even that has a predicate, for it is one; it is not pure essence. Must there not be something beyond that again, which is not even one, but is nameless, inconceivable, absolute? What an abyss! How shall the human mind find anything whereon to rest, in the vast nowhere between it and the object of its search? The search after the One issues in a wail to the innumerable; and kind gods, angels, and heroes, not human indeed, but still conceivable enough to satisfy at least the imagination, step in to fill the void, as they have done since, and may do again; and so, as Mr. Carlyle has it, "the bottomless pit got roofed over," as it may be again ere long.

Are we then to say, that Neoplatonism was a failure? That Alexandria, during four centuries of profound and earnest thought, added nothing? Heaven forbid that we should say so of a philosophy which has exercised on European thought, at the crisis of its noblest life and action, an influence as great as did the Aristotelian system during the Middle Ages. We must never forget, that during the two centuries which commence with the fall of Constantinople, and end with our civil wars, not merely almost all great thinkers, but courtiers, statesmen, warriors, poets, were more or less Neoplatonists. The Greek grammarians, who migrated into Italy, brought with them the works of Plotinus, Iamblichus, and Proclus; and their gorgeous reveries were welcomed eagerly by the European mind, just revelling in the free thought of youthful manhood. And yet the Alexandrian impotence for any practical and social purposes was to be manifested, as utterly as it was in Alexandria or in Athens of old. Ficinus and Picus of Mirandola worked no deliverance, either for Italian morals or polity, at a time when such deliverance was needed bitterly enough. Neoplatonism was petted by luxurious and heathen popes, as an elegant play of the cultivated fancy, which could do their real power, their practical system, neither good nor harm. And one cannot help feeling, while reading the magnificent oration on Supra-sensual Love, which Castiglione, in his admirable book "The Courtier," puts into the mouth of the profligate Bembo, how near mysticism may lie not merely to dilettantism or to Pharisaism, but to sensuality itself. But in England, during Elizabeth's reign, the practical weakness of Neoplatonism was compensated by the noble practical life which men were compelled to live in those great times; by the strong hold which they had of the ideas of family and national life, of law and personal faith. And I cannot but believe it to have been a mighty gain to such men as Sidney, Raleigh, and Spenser, that they had drunk, however slightly, of the wells of Proclus and Plotinus. One cannot read Spenser's "Fairy Queen," above all his Garden of Adonis, and his cantos on Mutability, without feeling that his Neoplatonism must have kept him safe from many a dark eschatological superstition, many a narrow and bitter dogmatism, which was even then tormenting the English mind, and must have helped to give him altogether a freer and more loving conception, if not a consistent or accurate one, of the wondrous harmony of that mysterious analogy between the physical and the spiritual, which alone makes poetry (and I had almost said philosophy also) possible, and have taught him to behold alike in suns and planets, in flowers and insects, in man and in beings higher than man, one glorious order of love and wisdom, linking them all to Him from whom they all proceed, rays from His cloudless sunlight, mirrors of His eternal glory.

But as the Elizabethan age, exhausted by its own fertility, gave place to the Caroline, Neoplatonism ran through much the same changes. It was good for us, after all, that the plain strength of the Puritans, unphilosophical as they were, swept it away. One feels in reading the later Neoplatonists, Henry More, Smith, even Cudworth (valuable as he is), that the old accursed distinction between the philosopher, the scholar, the illuminate, and the plain righteous man, was growing up again very fast. The school from which the "Religio Medici" issued was not likely to make any bad men good, or any foolish men wise.

Besides, as long as men were continuing to quote poor old Proclus as an irrefragable authority, and believing that he, forsooth, represented the sense of Plato, the new-born Baconian philosophy had but little chance in the world. Bacon had been right in his dislike of Platonism years before, though he was unjust to Plato himself. It was Proclus whom he was really reviling; Proclus as Plato's commentator and representative. The lion had for once got into the ass's skin, and was treated accordingly. The true Platonic method, that dialectic which the Alexandrians gradually abandoned, remains yet to be tried, both in England and in Germany; and I am much mistaken, if, when fairly used, it be not found the ally, not the enemy, of the Baconian philosophy; in fact, the inductive method applied to words, as the expressions of Metaphysic Laws, instead of to natural phenomena, as the expressions of Physical ones. If you wish to see the highest instances of this method, read Plato himself, not Proclus. If you wish to see how the same method can be applied to Christian truth, read the dialectic passages in Augustine's "Confessions." Whether or not you shall agree with their conclusions, you will not be likely, if you have a truly scientific habit of mind, to complain that they want either profundity, severity, or simplicity.

So concludes the history of one of the Alexandrian schools of Metaphysic. What was the fate of the other is a subject which I must postpone to my next Lecture.

LECTURE IV--THE CROSS AND THE CRESCENT

I tried to point out, in my last Lecture, the causes which led to the decay of the Pagan metaphysic of Alexandria. We have now to consider the fate of the Christian school.

You may have remarked that I have said little or nothing about the positive dogmas of Clement, Origen, and their disciples; but have only brought out the especial points of departure between them and the Heathens. My reason for so doing was twofold: first, I could not have examined them without entering on controversial ground; next, I am very desirous to excite some of my hearers, at least, to examine these questions for themselves.

I entreat them not to listen to the hasty sneer to which many of late have given way, that the Alexandrian divines were mere mystics, who corrupted Christianity by an admixture of Oriental and Greek thought. My own belief is that they expanded and corroborated Christianity, in spite of great errors and defects on certain points, far more than they corrupted it; that they presented it to the minds of cultivated and scientific men in the only form in which it would have satisfied their philosophic aspirations, and yet contrived, with wonderful wisdom, to ground their philosophy on the very same truths which they taught to the meanest slaves, and to appeal in the philosophers to the same inward faculty to which they appealed in the slave; namely, to that inward eye, that moral sense and reason, whereby each and every man can, if he will, "judge of himself that which is right." I boldly say that I believe the Alexandrian Christians to have made the best, perhaps the only, attempt yet made by men, to proclaim a true world-philosophy; whereby I mean a philosophy common to all races, ranks, and intellects, embracing the whole phenomena of humanity, and not an arbitrarily small portion of them, and capable of being understood and appreciated by every human being from the highest to the lowest. And when you hear of a system of reserve in teaching, a *disciplina arcani*, of an esoteric and exoteric, an inner and outer school, among these men, you must not be frightened at the words, as if they spoke of priestcraft, or an intellectual aristocracy, who kept the kernel of the nut for themselves, and gave the husks to the mob. It was not so with the Christian schools; it was so with the Heathen ones. The Heathens were content that the mob, the herd, should have the husks. Their avowed intention and wish was to leave the herd, as they called them, in the mere outward observance of the old idolatries, while they themselves, the cultivated philosophers, had the monopoly of those deeper spiritual truths which were contained under the old superstitions, and were too sacred to be profaned by the vulgar eyes. The Christian method was the exact opposite. They boldly called those vulgar eyes to enter into the very holy of holies, and there gaze on the very deepest root-ideas of their philosophy. They owned no ground for their own speculations which was not common to the harlots and the slaves around. And this was what enabled them to do this; this was what brought on them the charge of demagogism, the hatred of philosophers, the persecution of princes--that their ground was a moral ground, and not a merely intellectual one; that they started, not from any notions of the understanding, but from the inward conscience, that truly pure Reason in which the intellectual and the moral spheres are united, which they believed to exist, however dimmed or crushed, in every human being, capable of being awakened, purified, and raised up to a noble and heroic life. They concealed nothing moral from their disciples: only they forbade them to meddle with intellectual matters, before they had had a regular intellectual training. The witnesses of reason and conscience were sufficient guides for all men, and at them the many might well stop short. The teacher only needed to proceed further, not into a higher region, but into a lower one, namely, into the region of the logical understanding, and there make deductions from, and illustrations of, those higher truths which he held in common with every slave, and held on the same ground as they.

And the consequence of this method of philosophising was patent. They were enabled to produce, in the lives of millions, generation after generation, a more immense moral improvement than the world had ever seen before. Their disciples did actually become righteous and good men, just in proportion as they were true to the lessons they learnt. They did, for centuries, work a distinct and palpable deliverance on the earth; while all the solemn and earnest meditation of the Neoplatonists, however good or true, worked no deliverance whatsoever. Plotinus longed at one time to make a practical attempt. He asked the Emperor Gallienus, his patron, to rebuild for him a city in Campania; to allow him to call it Platonopolis, and put it into the hands of him and his disciples, that they might there realise Plato's ideal republic. Luckily for the reputation of Neoplatonism, the scheme was swamped by the courtiers of Gallienus, and the earth was saved the sad and ludicrous sight of a realised Laputa; probably a very quarrelsome one. That was his highest practical conception: the foundation of a new society: not the regeneration of society as it existed.

That work was left for the Christian schools; and up to a certain point they performed it. They made men good. This was the test, which of the schools was in the right: this was the test, which of the two had hold of the eternal roots of metaphysic. Cicero says, that he had learnt more philosophy from the Laws of the Twelve Tables than from all the Greeks. Clement and his school might have said the same of the Hebrew Ten Commandments and Jewish Law, which are so marvellously analogous to the old Roman laws, founded, as they are, on the belief in a Supreme Being, a Jupiter--literally a Heavenly Father--who is the source and the sanction of law; of whose justice man's justice is the pattern; who is the avenger of crimes against marriage, property, life; on whom depends the sanctity of an oath. And so, to compare great things with small, there was a truly practical human element here in the Christian teaching; purely ethical and metaphysical, and yet palpable to the simplest and lowest, which gave to it a regenerating force which the highest efforts of Neoplatonism could never attain.

And yet Alexandrian Christianity, notoriously enough, rotted away, and perished hideously. Most true. But what if the causes of its decay and death were owing to its being untrue to itself?

I do not say that they had no excuses for being untrue to their own faith. We are not here to judge them. That peculiar subtlety of mind, which rendered the Alexandrians the great thinkers of the then world, had with Christians, as well as Heathens, the effect of alluring them away from practice to speculation. The Christian school, as was to be expected from the moral ground of their philosophy, yielded to it far more slowly than the Heathen, but they did yield, and especially after they had conquered and expelled the Heathen school. Moreover, the long battle with the Heathen school had stirred up in them habits of exclusiveness, of denunciation; the spirit which cannot assert a fact, without dogmatising rashly and harshly on the consequences of denying that fact. Their minds assumed a permanent habit of combativeness. Having no more Heathens to fight, they began fighting each other, excommunicating each other; denying to all who differed from them any share of that light, to claim which for all men had been the very ground of their philosophy. Not that they would have refused the Logos to all men in words. They would have cursed a man for denying the existence of the Logos in every man; but they would have equally cursed him for acting on his existence in practice, and treating the heretic as one who had that within him to which a preacher might appeal. Thus they became Dogmatists; that is, men who assert a truth so fiercely, as to forget that a truth is meant to be used, and not merely asserted--if, indeed, the fierce assertion of a truth in frail man is not generally a sign of some secret doubt of it, and in inverse proportion to his practical living faith in it: just as he who is always telling you that he is a man, is not the most likely to behave like a man. And why did this befall them? Because they forgot practically that the light proceeded from a Person. They could argue over notions and dogmas deduced from the notion of His personality: but they were shut up in those notions; they had forgotten that if He was a Person, His eye was on them, His rule and kingdom within them; and that if He was a Person, He had a character, and that that character was a righteous and a loving character: and therefore they were not ashamed, in defending these notions and dogmas about Him, to commit acts abhorrent to His character, to lie, to slander, to intrigue, to hate, even to murder, for the sake of what they madly called His glory: but which was really only their own glory--the glory of their own dogmas; of propositions and conclusions in their own brain, which, true or false, were equally heretical in their mouths, because they used them only as watchwords of division. Orthodox or unorthodox, they lost the knowledge of God, for they lost the knowledge of righteousness, and love, and peace. That Divine Logos, and theology as a whole, receded further and further aloft into abysmal heights, as it became a mere dreary system of dead scientific terms, having no practical bearing on their hearts and lives; and then they, as the Neoplatonists had done before them, filled up the void by those daemonologies, images, base Fetish worships, which made the Mohammedan invaders regard them, and I believe justly, as polytheists and idolaters, base as the pagan Arabs of the desert.

I cannot but believe them, moreover, to have been untrue to the teaching of Clement and his school, in that coarse and materialist admiration of celibacy which ruined Alexandrian society, as their dogmatic ferocity ruined Alexandrian thought. The Creed which taught them that in the person of the Incarnate Logos, that which was most divine had been proved to be most human, that which was most human had been proved to be most divine, ought surely to have given to them, as it has given to modern Europe, nobler, clearer, simpler views of the true relation of the sexes. However, on this matter they did not see their way. Perhaps, in so debased an age, so profligate a world, as that out of which Christianity had risen, it was impossible to see the true beauty and sanctity of those primary bonds of humanity. And while the relation of the sexes was looked on in a wrong light, all other social relations were necessarily also misconceived. "The very ideas of family and national life," as it has been said, "those two divine roots of the Church, severed from which she is certain to wither away into that most cruel and most godless of spectres, a religious world, had perished in the East, from the evil influence of the universal practice of slave- holding, as well as from the degradation of that Jewish nation which had been for ages the great witness for these ideas; and all classes, like their forefather Adam--like, indeed, the Old Adam--the selfish, cowardly, brute nature in every man and in every age--were shifting the blame of sin from their own consciences to human relationships and duties, and therein, to the God who had appointed them; and saying, as of old, 'The woman whom Thou gavest to be with me, she gave me of the tree, and I did eat.'"

Much as Christianity did, even in Egypt, for woman, by asserting her moral and spiritual equality with the man, there seems to have been no suspicion that she was the true complement of the man, not merely by softening him, but by strengthening him; that true manhood can be no more developed without the influence of the woman, than true womanhood without the influence of the man. There is no trace among the Egyptian celibates of that chivalrous woman-worship which our Gothic forefathers brought with them into the West, which shed a softening and ennobling light round the mediaeval convent life, and warded off for centuries the worst effects of monasticism. Among the religious of Egypt, the monk regarded the nun, the nun the monk, with dread and aversion; while both looked on the married population of the opposite sex with a coarse contempt and disgust which is hardly credible, did not the foul records of it stand written to this day, in Rosweyde's extraordinary "Vitae Patrum Eremiticorum;" no barren school of metaphysic, truly, for those who are philosophic enough to believe that all phenomena whatsoever of the human mind are worthy matter for scientific induction.

And thus grew up in Egypt a monastic world, of such vastness that it was said to equal in number the laity. This produced, no doubt, an enormous increase in the actual amount of moral evil. But it produced three other effects, which were the ruin of Alexandria. First, a continually growing enervation and numerical decrease of the population; next, a carelessness of, and contempt for social and political life; and lastly, a most brutalising effect on the lay population; who, told that they were, and believing themselves to be, beings of a lower order, and living by a lower standard, sank down more and more generation after generation. They were of the world, and the ways of the world they must follow. Political life had no inherent sanctity or nobleness; why act holily and nobly in it? Family life had no inherent sanctity or nobleness; why act holily and nobly in it either, if there were no holy, noble, and divine principle or ground for it? And thus grew up, both in Egypt, Syria, and Byzantium, a chaos of profligacy and chicanery, in rulers and people, in the home and the market, in the theatre and the senate, such as the world has rarely seen before or since; a chaos which reached its culmination in the seventh century, the age of Justinian and Theodora, perhaps the two most hideous sovereigns, worshipped by the most hideous empire of parasites and hypocrites, cowards and wantons, that ever insulted the long-suffering of a righteous God.

But, for Alexandria at least, the cup was now full. In the year 640 the Alexandrians were tearing each other in pieces about some Jacobite and Melchite controversy, to me incomprehensible, to you unimportant, because the fighters on both sides seem to have lost (as all parties do in their old age) the knowledge of what they were fighting for, and to have so bewildered the question with personal intrigues, spites, and quarrels, as to make it nearly as enigmatic as that famous contemporary war between the blue and green factions at Constantinople, which began by backing in the theatre, the charioteers who drove in blue dresses, against those wild drove in green; then went on to identify themselves each with one of the prevailing theological factions; gradually developed, the one into an aristocratic, the other into a democratic, religious party; and ended by a civil war in the streets of Constantinople, accompanied by the most horrible excesses, which had nearly, at one time, given up the city to the flames, and driven Justinian from his throne.

In the midst of these Jacobite and Melchite controversies and riots, appeared before the city the armies of certain wild and unlettered Arab tribes. A short and fruitless struggle followed; and, strange to say, a few months swept away from the face of the earth, not only the wealth, the commerce, the castles, and the liberty, but the philosophy and the Christianity of Alexandria; crushed to powder by one fearful blow, all that had been built up by Alexander and the Ptolemies, by Clement and the philosophers, and made void, to all appearance, nine hundred years of human toil. The people, having no real hold on their hereditary Creed, accepted, by tens of thousands, that of the Mussulman invaders. The Christian remnant became tributaries; and Alexandria dwindled, from that time forth, into a petty seaport town.

And now--can we pass over this new metaphysical school of Alexandria? Can we help inquiring in what the strength of Islamism lay? I, at least, cannot. I cannot help feeling that I am bound to examine in what relation the creed of Omar and Amrou stands to the Alexandrian speculations of five hundred years, and how it had power to sweep those speculations utterly from the Eastern mind. It is a difficult problem; to me, as a Christian priest, a very awful problem. What more awful historic problem, than to see the lower creed destroying the higher? to see God, as it were, undoing his own work, and repenting Him that He had made man? Awful indeed: but I can honestly say, that it is one from the investigation of which I have learnt--I cannot yet tell how much: and of this I am sure, that without that old Alexandrian philosophy, I should not have been able to do justice to Islam; without Islam I should not have been able to find in that Alexandrian philosophy, an ever-living and practical element.

I must, however, first entreat you to dismiss from your minds the vulgar notion that Mohammed was in anywise a bad man, or a conscious deceiver, pretending to work miracles, or to do things which he did not do. He sinned in one instance: but, as far as I can see, only in that one--I mean against what he must have known to be right. I allude to his relaxing in his own case those wise restrictions on polygamy which he had proclaimed. And yet, even in this case, the desire for a child may have been the true cause of his weakness. He did not see the whole truth, of course: but he was an infinitely better man than the men around: perhaps, all in all, one of the best men of his day. Many here may have read Mr. Carlyle's vindication of

Mohammed in his Lectures on Hero Worship; to those who have not, I shall only say, that I entreat them to do so; and that I assure them, that though I differ in many things utterly from Mr. Carlyle's inferences and deductions in that lecture, yet that I am convinced, from my own acquaintance with the original facts and documents, that the picture there drawn of Mohammed is a true and a just description of a much-calumniated man.

Now, what was the strength of Islam? The common answer is, fanaticism and enthusiasm. To such answers I can only rejoin: Such terms must be defined before they are used, and we must be told what fanaticism and enthusiasm are. Till then I have no more e priori respect for a long word ending in -ism or -asm than I have for one ending in -ation or - ality. But while fanaticism and enthusiasm are being defined--a work more difficult than is commonly fancied--we will go on to consider another answer. We are told that the strength of Islam lay in the hope of their sensuous Paradise and fear of their sensuous Gehenna. If so, this is the first and last time in the world's history that the strength of any large body of people--perhaps of any single man--lay in such a hope. History gives us innumerable proofs that such merely selfish motives are the parents of slavish impotence, of pedantry and conceit, of pious frauds, often of the most devilish cruelty: but, as far as my reading extends, of nothing better. Moreover, the Christian Greeks had much the same hopes on those points as the Mussulmans; and similar causes should produce similar effects: but those hopes gave them no strength. Besides, according to the Mussulmans' own account, this was not their great inspiring idea; and it is absurd to consider the wild battle-cries of a few imaginative youths, about black-eyed and green- kerchiefed Houris calling to them from the skies, as representing the average feelings of a generation of sober and self-restraining men, who showed themselves actuated by far higher motives.

Another answer, and one very popular now, is that the Mussulmans were strong, because they believed what they said; and the Greeks weak, because they did not believe what they said. From this notion I shall appeal to another doctrine of the very same men who put it forth, and ask them, Can any man be strong by believing a lie? Have you not told us, nobly enough, that every lie is by its nature rotten, doomed to death, certain to prove its own impotence, and be shattered to atoms the moment you try to use it, to bring it into rude actual contact with fact, and Nature, and the eternal laws? Faith to be strong must be faith in something which is not one's self; faith in something eternal, something objective, something true, which would exist just as much though we and all the world disbelieved it. The strength of belief comes from that which is believed in; if you separate it from that, it becomes a mere self-opinion, a sensation of positiveness; and what sort of strength that will give, history will tell us in the tragedies of the Jews who opposed Titus, of the rabble who followed Walter the Penniless to the Crusades, of the Munster Anabaptists, and many another sad page of human folly. It may give the fury of idiots; not the deliberate might of valiant men. Let us pass this by, then; believing that faith can only give strength where it is faith in something true and right: and go on to another answer almost as popular as the last.

We are told that the might of Islam lay in a certain innate force and savage virtue of the Arab character. If we have discovered this in the followers of Mohammed, they certainly had not discovered it in themselves. They spoke of themselves, rightly or wrongly, as men who had received a divine light, and that light a moral light, to teach them to love that which was good, and refuse that which was evil; and to that divine light they stedfastly and honestly attributed every right action of their lives. Most noble and affecting, in my eyes, is that answer of Saad's aged envoy to Yezdegird, king of Persia, when he reproached him with the past savagery and poverty of the Arabs. "Whatsoever thou hast said," answered the old man, "regarding the former condition of the Arabs is true. Their food was green lizards; they buried their infant daughters alive; nay, some of them feasted on dead carcases, and drank blood; while others slew their kinsfolk, and thought themselves great and valiant, when by so doing they became possessed of more property. They were clothed with hair garments, they knew not good from evil, and made no distinction between that which was lawful and unlawful. Such was our state; but God in his mercy has sent us, by a holy prophet, a sacred volume, which teaches us the true faith."

These words, I think, show us the secret of Islam. They are a just comment on that short and rugged chapter of the Koran which is said to have been Mohammed's first attempt either at prophecy or writing; when, after long fasting and meditation among the desert hills, under the glorious eastern stars, he came down and told his good Kadijah that he had found a great thing, and that she must help him to write it down. And what was this which seemed to the unlettered camel-driver so price-less a treasure? Not merely that God was one God--vast as that discovery was--but that he was a God "who showeth to man the thing which he knew not;" a "most merciful God;" a God, in a word, who could be trusted; a God who would teach and strengthen; a God, as he said, who would give him courage to set his face like a flint, and would put an answer in his mouth when his idolatrous countrymen cavilled and sneered at his message to them, to turn from their idols of wood and stone, and become righteous men, as Abraham their forefather was righteous.

"A God who showeth to man the thing which he knew not." That idea gave might to Islam, because it was a real idea, an eternal fact; the result of a true insight into the character of God. And that idea alone, believe me, will give conquering might either to creed, philosophy, or heart of man. Each will be strong, each will endure, in proportion as it believes that God is one who shows to man the thing which he knew not: as it believes, in short, in that Logos of which Saint John wrote, that He was the light who lightens every man who comes into the world.

In a word, the wild Koreish had discovered, more or less clearly, that end and object of all metaphysic whereof I have already spoken so often; that external and imperishable beauty for which Plato sought of old; and had seen that its name was righteousness, and that it dwelt absolutely in an absolutely righteous person; and moreover, that this person was no careless self-contented epicurean deity; but that He was, as they loved to call Him, the most merciful God; that He cared for men; that He desired to make men righteous. Of that they could not doubt. The fact was palpable, historic, present. To them the degraded Koreish of the desert, who as they believed, and I think believed rightly, had fallen from the old Monotheism of their forefathers Abraham and Ismael, into the lowest fetishism, and with that into the lowest brutality and wretchedness--to them, while they were making idols of wood and stone; eating dead carcases; and burying their daughters alive; careless of chastity, of justice, of property; sunk in unnatural crimes. dead in trespasses and sins; hateful and hating one another--a man, one of their own people had come, saying: "I have a message from the one righteous God. His curse is on all this, for it is unlike Himself. He will have you righteous men, after the pattern of your fore-father Abraham. Be that, and arise, body, soul, and spirit, out of your savagery and brutishness. Then you shall be able to trample under font the profligate idolaters, to sweep the Greek tyrants from the land which they have been oppressing for centuries, and to recover the East for its rightful heirs, the children of Abraham." Was this not, in every sense, a message from God? I must deny the philosophy of Clement and Augustine, I must deny my own conscience, my own reason, I must outrage my own moral sense, and confess that I have no immutable standard of right, that I know no eternal source of right, if I deny it to have been one; if I deny what seems to me the palpable historic fact, that those wild Koreish had in them a reason and a conscience, which could awaken to that message, and perceive its boundless beauty, its boundless importance, and that they did accept that message, and lived by it in proportion as they received it fully, such lives as no men in those times, and few in after times, have been able to live. If I feel, as I do feel, that Abubekr, Omar, Abu Obeidah, and Amrou, were better men than I am, I must throw away all that Philo--all that a Higher authority--has taught me: or I must attribute their lofty virtues to the one source of all in man which is not selfishness, and fancy, and fury, and blindness as of the beasts which perish.

Why, then, has Islamism become one of the most patent and complete failures upon earth, if the true test of a system's success be the gradual progress and amelioration of the human beings who are under its influence? First, I believe, from its allowing polygamy. I do not judge Mohammed for having allowed it. He found it one of the ancestral and immemorial customs of his nation. He found it throughout the Hebrew Scriptures. He found it in the case of Abraham, his ideal man; and, as he believed, the divinely-inspired ancestor of his race. It seemed to him that what was right for Abraham, could not be wrong for an Arab. God shall judge him, not I. Moreover, the Christians of the East, divided into either monks or profligates; and with far lower and more brutal notions of the married state than were to be found in Arab poetry and legend, were the very last men on earth to make him feel the eternal and divine beauty of that pure wedded love which Christianity has not only proclaimed, but commanded, and thereby emancipated woman from her old slavery to the stronger sex. And I believe, from his chivalrous faithfulness to his good wife Kadijah, as long as she lived, that Mohammed was a man who could have accepted that great truth in all its fulness, had he but been taught it. He certainly felt the evil of polyamy so strongly as to restrict it in every possible way, except the only right way--namely, the proclamation of the true ideal of marriage. But his ignorance, mistake, sin, if you will, was a deflection from the right law, from the true constitution of man, and therefore it avenged itself. That chivalrous respect for woman, which was so strong in the early Mohammedans, died out. The women themselves--who, in the first few years of Islamism, rose as the men rose, and became their helpmates, counsellors, and fellow-warriors--degenerated rapidly into mere playthings. I need not enter into the painful subject of woman's present position in the East, and the social consequences thereof. But I firmly believe, not merely as a theory, but as a fact which may be proved by abundant evidence, that to polygamy alone is owing nine-tenths of the present decay and old age of every Mussulman nation; and that till it be utterly abolished, all Western civilisation and capital, and all the civil and religious liberty on earth, will not avail one jot toward their revival. You must regenerate the family before you can regenerate the nation, and the relation of husband and wife before the family; because, as long as the root is corrupt, the fruit will be corrupt also.

But there is another cause of the failure of Islamism, more intimately connected with those metaphysical questions which we have been hitherto principally considering.

Among the first Mussulmans, as I have said, there was generally the most intense belief in each man that he was personally under a divine guide and teacher. But their creed contained nothing which could keep up that belief in the minds of succeeding generations. They had destroyed the good with the evil, and they paid the penalty of their undistinguishing wrath. In sweeping away the idolatries and fetish worships of the Syrian Catholics, the Mussulmans had swept away also that doctrine which alone can deliver men from idolatry and fetish worships--if not outward and material ones, yet the still more subtle, and therefore more dangerous idolatries of the intellect. For they had swept away the belief in the Logos; in a divine teacher of every human soul, who was, in some mysterious way, the pattern and antitype of human virtue and wisdom. And more, they had swept away that belief in the incarnation of the Logos, which alone can make man feel that his divine teacher is one who can enter into the human duties, sorrows, doubts, of each human spirit. And, therefore, when Mohammed and his personal friends were dead, the belief in a present divine teacher, on the whole, died with them; and the Mussulmans began to put the Koran in the place of Him of whom the Koran spoke. They began to worship the book--which after all is not a book, but only an irregular collection of Mohammed's meditations, and notes for sermons--with the most slavish and ridiculous idolatry. They fell into a cabbalism, and a superstitious reverence for the mere letters and words of the Koran, to which the cabbalism of the old Rabbis was moderate and rational. They surrounded it, and the history of Mohammed, with all ridiculous myths, and prodigies, and lying wonders, whereof the book itself contained not a word; and which Mohammed, during his existence, had denied and repudiated, saying that he worked no miracles, and that none were needed; because only reason was required to show a man the hand of a good God in all human affairs. Nevertheless, these later Mussulmans found the miracles neces- sary to confirm their faith: and why? Because they had lost the sense of a present God, a God of order; and therefore hankered, as men in such a mood always will, after prodigious and unnatural proofs of His having been once present with their founder Mohammed.

And in the meanwhile that absolute and omnipotent Being whom Mohammed, arising out of his great darkness, had so nobly preached to the Koreish, receded in the minds of their descendants to an unapproachable and abysmal distance. For they had lost the sense of His present guidance, His personal care. They had lost all which could connect Him with the working of their own souls, with their human duties and struggles, with the belief that His mercy and love were counterparts of human mercy and human love; in plain English, that He was loving and merciful at all. The change came very gradually, thank God; you may read of noble sayings and deeds here and there, for many centuries after Mohammed: but it came; and then their belief in God's omnipotence and absoluteness dwindled into the most dark, and slavish, and benumbing fatalism. His unchangeableness became in their minds not an unchangeable purpose to teach, forgive, and deliver men--as it seemed to Mohammed to have been-- but a mere brute necessity, an unchangeable purpose to have His own way, whatsoever that way might be. That dark fatalism, also, has helped toward the decay of the Mohammedan nations. It has made them careless of self-improvement; faithless of the possibility of progress; and has kept, and will keep, the Mohammedan nations, in all intellectual matters, whole ages behind the Christian nations of the West.

How far the story of Omar's commanding the baths of Alexandria to be heated with the books from the great library is true, we shall never know. Some have doubted the story altogether: but so many fresh corroborations of it are said to have been lately discovered, in Arabic writers, that I can hardly doubt that it had some foundation in fact. One cannot but believe that John Philoponus, the last of the Alexandrian grammarians, when he asked his patron Amrou the gift of the library, took care to save some, at least, of its treasures; and howsoever strongly Omar may have felt or said that all books which agreed with the Koran were useless, and all which disagreed with it only fit to be destroyed, the general feeling of the Mohammedan leaders was very different. As they settled in the various countries which they conquered, education seems to have been considered by them an important object. We even find some of them, in the same generation as Mohammed, obeying strictly the Prophet's command to send all captive children to school--a fact which speaks as well for the Mussulmans' good sense, as it speaks ill for the state of education among the degraded descendants of the Greek conquerors of the East. Gradually philosophic Schools arose, first at Bagdad, and then at Cordova; and the Arabs carried on the task of commenting on Aristotle's Logic, and Ptolemy's Megiste Syntaxis--which last acquired from them the name of Almagest, by which it was so long known during the Middle Ages.

But they did little but comment, though there was no Neoplatonic or mystic element in their commentaries. It seems as if Alexandria was preordained, by its very central position, to be the city of commentators, not of originators. It is worthy of remark, that Philoponus, who may be considered as the man who first introduced the simple warriors of the Koreish to the treasures of Greek thought, seems to have been the first rebel against the Neoplatonist eclecticism. He maintained, and truly, that Porphyry, Proclus, and the rest, had entirely misunderstood Aristotle, when they attempted to reconcile him with Plato, or incorporate his philosophy into Platonism. Aristotle was henceforth the text-book of Arab savants. It was natural enough. The Mussulman mind was trained in habits of absolute obedience to the authority of fixed dogmas. All those attempts to follow out metaphysic to its highest object, theology, would be useless if not wrong in the eyes of a Mussulman, who had already his simple and sharply-defined creed on all matters relating to the unseen world. With him metaphysic was a study altogether divorced from man's higher life and aspirations. So also were physics. What need had he of Cosmogonies? what need to trace the relations between man and the universe, or the universe and its Maker? He had his definite material Elysium and Tartarus, as the only ultimate relation between man and the universe; his dogma of an absolute fiat, creating arbitrary and once for all, as the only relation between the universe and its Maker: and further it was not lawful to speculate. The idea which I believe unites both physic and metaphysic with man's highest inspirations and widest speculations--the Alexandria idea of the Logos, of the Deity working in time and space by successive thoughts--he had not heard of; for it was dead, as I have said, in Alexandria itself; and if he had heard of it, he would have spurned it as detracting from the absoluteness of that abysmal one Being, of whom he so nobly yet so partially bore witness. So it was to be; doubtless it was right that it should be so. Man's eye is too narrow to see a whole truth, his brain too weak to carry a whole truth. Better for him, and better for the world, is perhaps the method on which man has been educated in every age, by which to each school, or party, or nation, is given some one great truth, which they are to work out to its highest development, to exemplify in actual life, leaving some happier age-- perhaps, alas! only some future state--to reconcile that too favoured dogma with other truths which lie beside it, and without which it is always incomplete, and sometimes altogether barren.

But such schools of science, founded on such a ground as this, on the mere instinct of curiosity, had little chance of originality or vitality. All the great schools of the world, the elder Greek philosophy, the Alexandrian, the present Baconian school of physics, have had a deeper motive for their search, a far higher object which they hope to discover. But indeed, the Mussulmans did not so much wish to discover truth, as to cultivate their own intellects. For that purpose a sharp and subtle systematist, like Aristotle, was the very man whom they required; and from the destruction of Alexandria may date the rise of the Aristotelian philosophy. Translations of his works were made into Arabic, first, it is said, from Persian and Syriac translations; the former of which had been made during the sixth and seventh centuries, by the wreck of the Neoplatonist party, during their visit to the philosophic Chozroos. A century after, they filled Alexandria. After them Almansoor, Hairoun Alraschid, and their successors, who patronised the Nestorian Christians, obtained from them translations of the philosophic, medical, and astronomical Greek works; while the last of the Omniades, Abdalrahman, had introduced the same literary taste into Spain, where, in the thirteenth century, Averroes and Maimonides rivalled the fame of Avicenna, who had flourished at Bagdad a century before.

But, as I have said already, these Arabs seem to have invented nothing; they only commented. And yet not only commented; for they preserved for us those works of whose real value they were so little aware. Averroes, in quality of commentator on Aristotle, became his rival in the minds of the mediaeval schoolmen; Avicenna, in quality of commentator on Hippocrates and Galen, was for centuries the text-book of all European physicians; while Albatani and Aboul Wefa, as astronomers, commented on Ptolemy, not however without making a few important additions to his knowledge; for Aboul Wefa discovered a third inequality of the moon's motion, in addition to the two mentioned by Ptolemy, which he did, according to Professor Whewell, in a truly philosophic manner--an apparently solitary instance, and one which, in its own day, had no effect; for the fact was forgotten, and rediscovered centuries after by Tycho Brahe. To Albatani, however, we owe two really valuable heirlooms. The one is the use of the sine, or half-chord of the double arc, instead of the chord of the arc itself, which had been employed by the Greek astronomers; the other, of even more practical benefit, was the introduction of the present decimal arithmetic, instead of the troublesome sexagesimal arithmetic of the Greeks. These ten digits, however, seem, says Professor Whewell, by the confession of the Arabians themselves, to be of Indian origin, and thus form no exception to the sterility of the Arabian genius in scientific inventions. Nevertheless we are bound, in all fairness, to set against his condemnation of the Arabs Professor De Morgan's opinion of the Moslem, in his article on Euclid: "Some writers speak slightingly of this progress, the results of which they are too apt to compare with those of our own time. They ought rather to place the Saracens by the side of their own Gothic ancestors; and making some allowance for the more advantageous circumstances under which the first started, they should view the second systematically dispersing the remains of Greek civilisation, while the first were concentrating the geometry of Alexandria, the arithmetic and algebra of India, and the astronomy of both, to form a nucleus for the present state of science."

To this article of Professor De Morgan's on Euclid, {2} and to Professor Whewell's excellent "History of the Inductive Sciences," from which I, being neither Arabic scholar nor astronomer, have drawn most of my facts about physical science, I must refer those who wish to know more of the early rise of physics, and of their preservation by the Arabs, till a great and unexpected event brought them back again to the quarter of the globe where they had their birth, and where alone they could be regenerated into a new and practical life.

That great event was the Crusades. We have heard little of Alexandria lately. Its intellectual glory had departed westward and eastward, to Cordova and to Bagdad; its commercial greatness had left it for Cairo and Damietta. But Egypt was still the centre of communication between the two great stations of the Moslem power, and indeed, as Mr. Lane has shown in his most valuable translation of the "Arabian Nights," possessed a peculiar life and character of its own.

It was the rash object of the Crusaders to extinguish that life. Palestine was their first point of attack: but the later Crusaders seem to have found, like the rest of the world, that the destinies of Palestine could not be separated from those of Egypt; and to Damietta, accordingly, was directed that last disastrous attempt of St. Louis, which all may read so graphically described in the pages of Joinville.

The Crusaders failed utterly of the object at which they aimed. They succeeded in an object of which they never dreamed; for in those Crusades the Moslem and the Christian had met face to face, and found that both were men, that they had a common humanity, a common eternal standard of nobleness and virtue. So the Christian knights went home humbler and wiser men, when they found in the Saracen emirs the same generosity, truth, mercy, chivalrous self-sacrifice, which they had fancied their own peculiar possession, and added to that, a civilisation and a learning which they could only admire and imitate. And thus, from the era of the Crusades, a kindlier feeling sprang up between the Crescent and the Cross, till it was again broken by the fearful invasions of the Turks throughout Eastern Europe. The learning of the Moslem, as well as their commerce, began to pour rapidly into Christendom, both from Spain, Egypt, and Syria; and thus the Crusaders were, indeed, rewarded according to their deeds. They had fancied that they were bound to vindicate the possession of the earth for Him to whom they believed the earth belonged. He showed them--or rather He has shown us, their children--that He can vindicate His own dominion better far than man can do it for Him; and their cruel and unjust aim was utterly foiled. That was not the way to make men know or obey Him. They took the sword, and perished by the sword. But the truly noble element in them--the element which our hearts and reasons recognise and love, in spite of all the loud words about the folly and fanaticism of the Crusades, whensoever we read "The Talisman" or "Ivanhoe"--the element of loyal faith and self-sacrifice--did not go unrequited. They learnt wider, juster views of man and virtue, which I cannot help believing must have had great effect in weakening in their minds their old, exclusive, and bigoted notions, and in paving the way for the great outburst of free thought, and the great assertion of the dignity of humanity, which the fifteenth century beheld. They opened a path for that influx of scientific knowledge which has produced, in after centuries, the most enormous effects on the welfare of Europe, and made life possible for millions who would otherwise have been pent within the narrow bounds of Europe, to devour each other in the struggle for room and bread.

But those Arabic translations of Greek authors were a fatal gift for Egypt, and scarcely less fatal gift for Bagdad. In that Almagest of Ptolemy, in that Organon of Aristotle, which the Crusaders are said to have brought home, lay, rude and embryotic, the germs of that physical science, that geographical knowledge which has opened to the European the commerce and the colonisation of the globe. Within three hundred years after his works reached Europe, Ptolemy had taught the Portuguese to sail round Africa; and from that day the stream of eastern wealth flowed no longer through the Red Sea, or the Persian Gulf, on its way to the new countries of the West; and not only Alexandria, but Damietta and Bagdad, dwindled down to their present insignificance. And yet the whirligig of time brings about its revenges. The stream of commerce is now rapidly turning back to its old channel; and British science bids fair to make Alexandria once more the inn of all the nations.

It is with a feeling of awe that one looks upon the huge possibilities of her future. Her own physical capacities, as the great mind of Napoleon saw, are what they always have been, inexhaustible; and science has learnt to set at naught the only defect of situation which has ever injured her prosperity, namely, the short land passage from the Nile to the Red Sea. The fate of Palestine is now more than ever bound up with her fate; and a British or French colony might, holding the two countries, develop itself into a nation as vast as sprang from Alexander's handful of Macedonians, and become the meeting point for the nations of the West and those great Anglo-Saxon peoples who seem destined to spring up in the Australian ocean. Wide as the dream may appear, steam has made it a far narrower one than the old actual fact, that for centuries the Phoenician and the Arabian interchanged at Alexandria the produce of Britain for that of Ceylon and Hindostan. And as for intellectual development, though Alexandria wants, as she has always wanted, that insular and exclusive position which seems almost necessary to develop original thought and original national life, yet she may still act as the point of fusion for distinct schools and polities, and the young and buoyant vigour of the new-born nations may at once teach, and learn from, the prudence, the experience, the traditional wisdom of the ancient Europeans.

This vision, however possible, may be a far-off one: but the first step towards it, at least, is being laid before our eyes--and that is, a fresh reconciliation between the Crescent and the Cross. Apart from all political considerations, which would be out of place here, I hail, as a student of philosophy, the school which is now, both in Alexandria and in Constantinople, teaching to Moslem and to Christians the same lesson which the Crusaders learnt in Egypt five hundred years ago. A few years' more perseverance in the valiant and righteous course which Britain has now chosen, will reward itself by opening a vast field for capital and enterprise, for the introduction of civil and religious liberty among the down-trodden peasantry of Egypt; as the Giaour becomes an object of respect, and trust, and gratitude to the Moslem; and as the feeling that Moslem and Giaour own a common humanity, a common eternal standard of justice and mercy, a common sacred obligation to perform our promises, and to succour the oppressed, shall have taken place of the old brute wonder at our careless audacity, and awkward assertion of power, which now expresses itself in the somewhat left-handed Alexandrian compliment--"There is one Satan, and there are many Satans: but there is no Satan like a Frank in a round hat."

It would be both uncourteous and unfair of me to close these my hasty Lectures, without expressing my hearty thanks for the great courtesy and kindness which I have received in this my first visit to your most noble and beautiful city; and often, I am proud to say, from those who differ from me deeply on many important points; and also for the attention with which I have been listened to while trying, clumsily enough, to explain dry and repulsive subjects, and to express opinions which may be new, and perhaps startling, to many of my hearers. If my imperfect hints shall have stirred up but one hearer to investigate this obscure and yet most important subject, and to examine for himself the original documents, I shall feel that my words in this place have not been spoken in vain; for even if such a seeker should arrive at conclusions different from my own (and I pretend to no infallibility), he will at least have learnt new facts, the parents of new thought, perhaps of new action; he will have come face to face with new human beings, in whom he will have been compelled to take a human interest; and will surely rise from his researches, let them lead him where they will, at least somewhat of a wider-minded and a wider-hearted man.

Notes:

{1} These Lectures were delivered at the Philosophical Institution, Edinburgh, in February, 1854, at the commencement of the Crimean War.

{2} Smith's "Classical Dictionary."

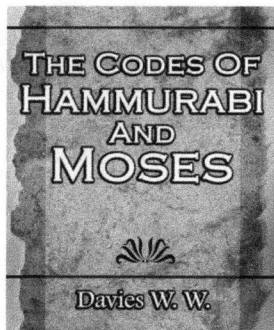

The Codes Of Hammurabi And Moses
W. W. Davies

QTY

The discovery of the Hammurabi Code is one of the greatest achievements of archaeology, and is of paramount interest, not only to the student of the Bible, but also to all those interested in ancient history...

Religion   **ISBN: *1-59462-338-4***   **Pages:132**

MSRP $12.95

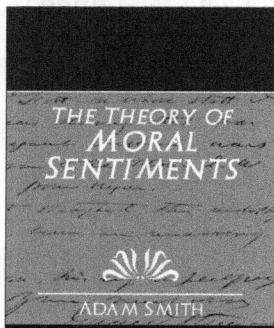

The Theory of Moral Sentiments
Adam Smith

QTY

This work from 1749. contains original theories of conscience amd moral judgment and it is the foundation for systemof morals.

Philosophy **ISBN: *1-59462-777-0***   **Pages:536**

MSRP $19.95

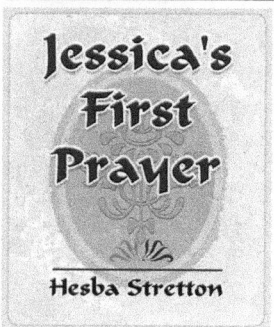

Jessica's First Prayer
Hesba Stretton

QTY

In a screened and secluded corner of one of the many railway-bridges which span the streets of London there could be seen a few years ago, from five o'clock every morning until half past eight, a tidily set-out coffee-stall, consisting of a trestle and board, upon which stood two large tin cans, with a small fire of charcoal burning under each so as to keep the coffee boiling during the early hours of the morning when the work-people were thronging into the city on their way to their daily toil...

Pages:84

Childrens   **ISBN: *1-59462-373-2***   *MSRP $9.95*

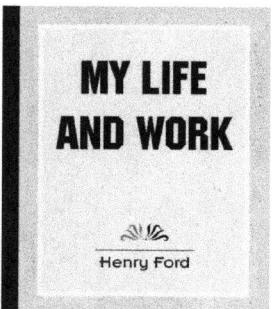

My Life and Work
Henry Ford

QTY

Henry Ford revolutionized the world with his implementation of mass production for the Model T automobile. Gain valuable business insight into his life and work with his own auto-biography... "We have only started on our development of our country we have not as yet, with all our talk of wonderful progress, done more than scratch the surface. The progress has been wonderful enough but..."

Pages:300

Biographies/   **ISBN: *1-59462-198-5***   *MSRP $21.95*

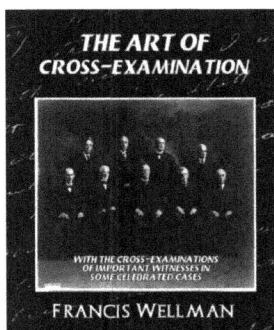

The Art of Cross-Examination
Francis Wellman

QTY

I presume it is the experience of every author, after his first book is published upon an important subject, to be almost overwhelmec with a wealth of ideas and illustrations which could readily have been included in his book, and which to his own mind, at least, seem to make a second edition inevitable. Such certainly was the case with me; and when the first edition had reached its sixth impression in five months, I rejoiced to learn that it seemed to my publishers that the book had met with a sufficiently favorable reception to justify a second and considerably enlarged edition. ..

Pages:412

Reference   ISBN: *1-59462-647-2*   *MSRP $19.95*

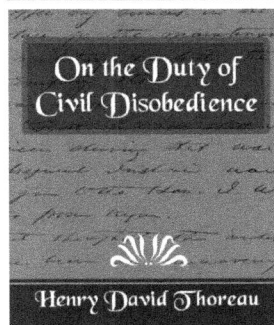

On the Duty of Civil Disobedience
Henry David Thoreau

QTY

Thoreau wrote his famous essay, On the Duty of Civil Disobedience, as a protest against an unjust but popular war and the immoral but popular institution of slave-owning. He did more than write—he declined to pay his taxes, and was hauled off to gaol in consequence. Who can say how much this refusal of his hastened the end of the war and cf slavery ?

Pages:48

Law   ISBN: *1-59462-747-9*   *MSRP $7.45*

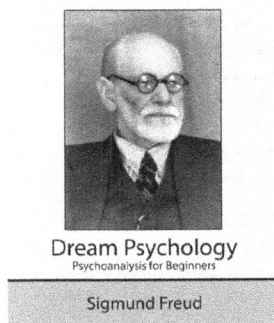

Dream Psychology Psychoanalysis for Beginners
Sigmund Freud

QTY

Sigmund Freud, born Sigismund Schlomo Freud (May 6, 1856 - September 23, 1939), was a Jewish-Austrian neurologist and psychiatrist who co-founded the psychoanalytic school of psychology. Freud is best known for his theories of the unconscious mind, especially involving the mechanism of repression; his redefinition of sexual desire as mobile and directed towards a wide variety of objects; and his therapeutic techniques, especially his understanding of transference in the therapeutic relationship and the presumed value of dreams as sources of insight into unconscious desires.

Pages:196

Psychology   ISBN: *1-59462-905-6*   *MSRP $15.45*

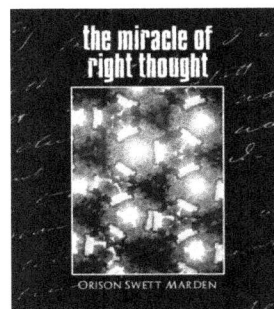

The Miracle of Right Thought
Orison Swett Marden

QTY

Believe with all of your heart that you will do what you were made to do. When the mind has once formed the habit of holding cheerful, happy, prosperous pictures, it will not be easy to form the opposite habit. It does not matter how improbable or how far away this realization may see, or how dark the prospects may be, if we visualize them as best we can, as vividly as possible, hold tenaciously to them and vigorously struggle to attain them, they will gradually become actualized, realized in the life. But a desire, a longing without endeavor, a yearning abandoned or held indifferently will vanish without realization.

Pages:360

Self Help   ISBN: *1-59462-644-8*   *MSRP $25.45*

www.bookjungle.com *email: sales@bookjungle.com fax: 630-214-0564 mail: Book Jungle PO Box 2226 Champaign, IL 61825*

QTY

The Rosicrucian Cosmo-Conception Mystic Christianity by *Max Heindel* ISBN: *1-59462-188-8* **$38.95**
The Rosicrucian Cosmo-conception is not dogmatic, neither does it appeal to any other authority than the reason of the student. It is: not controversial, but is: sent forth in the, hope that it may help to clear.. New Age/Religion Pages 646

Abandonment To Divine Providence by *Jean-Pierre de Caussade* ISBN: *1-59462-228-0* **$25.95**
"The Rev. Jean Pierre de Caussade was one of the most remarkable spiritual writers of the Society of Jesus in France in the 18th Century. His death took place at Toulouse in 1751. His works have gone through many editions and have been republished... Inspirational/Religion Pages 400

Mental Chemistry by *Charles Haanel* ISBN: *1-59462-192-6* **$23.95**
Mental Chemistry allows the change of material conditions by combining and appropriately utilizing the power of the mind. Much like applied chemistry creates something new and unique out of careful combinations of chemicals the mastery of mental chemistry... New Age Pages 354

The Letters of Robert Browning and Elizabeth Barret Barrett 1845-1846 vol II ISBN: *1-59462-193-4* **$35.95**
by *Robert Browning* and *Elizabeth Barrett* Biographies Pages 596

Gleanings In Genesis (volume I) by *Arthur W. Pink* ISBN: *1-59462-130-6* **$27.45**
Appropriately has Genesis been termed "the seed plot of the Bible" for in it we have, in germ form, almost all of the great doctrines which are afterwards fully developed in the books of Scripture which follow... Religion/Inspirational Pages 420

The Master Key by *L. W. de Laurence* ISBN: *1-59462-001-6* **$30.95**
In no branch of human knowledge has there been a more lively increase of the spirit of research during the past few years than in the study of Psychology, Concentration and Mental Discipline. The requests for authentic lessons in Thought Control, Mental Discipline and... New Age/Business Pages 422

The Lesser Key Of Solomon Goetia by *L. W. de Laurence* ISBN: *1-59462-092-X* **$9.95**
This translation of the first book of the "Lernegton" which is now for the first time made accessible to students of Talismanic Magic was done, after careful collation and edition, from numerous Ancient Manuscripts in Hebrew, Latin, and French... New Age/Occult Pages 92

Rubaiyat Of Omar Khayyam by *Edward Fitzgerald* ISBN:*1-59462-332-5* **$13.95**
Edward Fitzgerald, whom the world has already learned, in spite of his own efforts to remain within the shadow of anonymity, to look upon as one of the rarest poets of the century, was born at Bredfield, in Suffolk, on the 31st of March, 1809. He was the third son of John Purcell... Music Pages 172

Ancient Law by *Henry Maine* ISBN: *1-59462-128-4* **$29.95**
The chief object of the following pages is to indicate some of the earliest ideas of mankind, as they are reflected in Ancient Law, and to point out the relation of those ideas to modern thought. Religion/History Pages 452

Far-Away Stories by *William J. Locke* ISBN: *1-59462-129-2* **$19.45**
"Good wine needs no bush, but a collection of mixed vintages does. And this book is just such a collection. Some of the stories I do not want to remain buried for ever in the museum files of dead magazine-numbers an author's not unpardonable vanity..." Fiction Pages 272

Life of David Crockett by *David Crockett* ISBN: *1-59462-250-7* **$27.45**
"Colonel David Crockett was one of the most remarkable men of the times in which he lived. Born in humble life, but gifted with a strong will, an indomitable courage, and unremitting perseverance... Biographies/New Age Pages 424

Lip-Reading by *Edward Nitchie* ISBN: *1-59462-206-X* **$25.95**
Edward B. Nitchie, founder of the New York School for the Hard of Hearing, now the Nitchie School of Lip-Reading, Inc, wrote "LIP-READING Principles and Practice". The development and perfecting of this meritorious work on lip-reading was an undertaking... How-to Pages 400

A Handbook of Suggestive Therapeutics, Applied Hypnotism, Psychic Science ISBN: *1-59462-214-0* **$24.95**
by *Henry Munro* Health/New Age/Health/Self-help Pages 376

A Doll's House: and Two Other Plays by *Henrik Ibsen* ISBN: *1-59462-112-8* **$19.95**
Henrik Ibsen created this classic when in revolutionary 1848 Rome. Introducing some striking concepts in playwriting for the realist genre, this play has been studied the world over. Fiction/Classics/Plays 308

The Light of Asia by *sir Edwin Arnold* ISBN: *1-59462-204-3* **$13.95**
In this poetic masterpiece, Edwin Arnold describes the life and teachings of Buddha. The man who was to become known as Buddha to the world was born as Prince Gautama of India but he rejected the worldly riches and abandoned the reigns of power when... Religion/History/Biographies Pages 170

The Complete Works of Guy de Maupassant by *Guy de Maupassant* ISBN: *1-59462-157-8* **$16.95**
"For days and days, nights and nights, I had dreamed of that first kiss which was to consecrate our engagement, and I knew not on what spot I should put my lips..." Fiction/Classics Pages 240

The Art of Cross-Examination by *Francis L. Wellman* ISBN: *1-59462-309-0* **$26.95**
Written by a renowned trial lawyer, Wellman imparts his experience and uses case studies to explain how to use psychology to extract desired information through questioning. How-to/Science/Reference Pages 408

Answered or Unanswered? by *Louisa Vaughan* ISBN: *1-59462-248-5* **$10.95**
Miracles of Faith in China Religion Pages 112

The Edinburgh Lectures on Mental Science (1909) by *Thomas* ISBN: *1-59462-008-3* **$11.95**
This book contains the substance of a course of lectures recently given by the writer in the Queen Street Hall, Edinburgh. Its purpose is to indicate the Natural Principles governing the relation between Mental Action and Material Conditions... New Age/Psychology Pages 148

Ayesha by *H. Rider Haggard* ISBN: *1-59462-301-5* **$24.95**
Verily and indeed it is the unexpected that happens! Probably if there was one person upon the earth from whom the Editor of this, and of a certain previous history, did not expect to hear again... Classics Pages 380

Ayala's Angel by *Anthony Trollope* ISBN: *1-59462-352-X* **$29.95**
The two girls were both pretty, but Lucy who was twenty-one who supposed to be simple and comparatively unattractive, whereas Ayala was credited, as her Bombwhat romantic name might show, with poetic charm and a taste for romance. Ayala when her father died was nineteen... Fiction Pages 484

The American Commonwealth by *James Bryce* ISBN: *1-59462-286-8* **$34.45**
An interpretation of American democratic political theory. It examines political mechanics and society from the perspective of Scotsman James Bryce Politics Pages 572

Stories of the Pilgrims by *Margaret P. Pumphrey* ISBN: *1-59462-116-0* **$17.95**
This book explores pilgrims religious oppression in England as well as their escape to Holland and eventual crossing to America on the Mayflower, and their early days in New England... History Pages 268

QTY

The Fasting Cure *by Sinclair Upton*   ISBN: *1-59462-222-1*   **$13.95**
In the Cosmopolitan Magazine for May, 1910, and in the Contemporary Review (London) for April, 1910, I published an article dealing with my experiences in fasting. I have written a great many magazine articles, but never one which attracted so much attention... New Age/Self Help/Health Pages 164

Hebrew Astrology *by Sepharial*   ISBN: *1-59462-308-2*   **$13.45**
In these days of advanced thinking it is a matter of common observation that we have left many of the old landmarks behind and that we are now pressing forward to greater heights and to a wider horizon than that which represented the mind-content of our progenitors... Astrology Pages 144

Thought Vibration or The Law of Attraction in the Thought World   ISBN: *1-59462-127-6*   **$12.95**

by William Walker Atkinson   *Psychology/Religion Pages 144*

Optimism *by Helen Keller*   ISBN: *1-59462-108-X*   **$15.95**
Helen Keller was blind, deaf, and mute since 19 months old, yet famously learned how to overcome these handicaps, communicate with the world, and spread her lectures promoting optimism. An inspiring read for everyone... Biographies/Inspirational Pages 84

Sara Crewe *by Frances Burnett*   ISBN: *1-59462-360-0*   **$9.45**
In the first place, Miss Minchin lived in London. Her home was a large, dull, tall one, in a large, dull square, where all the houses were alike, and all the sparrows were alike, and where all the door-knockers made the same heavy sound... Childrens/Classic Pages 88

The Autobiography of Benjamin Franklin *by Benjamin Franklin*   ISBN: *1-59462-135-7*   **$24.95**
The Autobiography of Benjamin Franklin has probably been more extensively read than any other American historical work, and no other book of its kind has had such ups and downs of fortune. Franklin lived for many years in England, where he was agent... Biographies/History Pages 332

Name	
Email	
Telephone	
Address	
City, State ZIP	

☐ **Credit Card**   ☐ **Check / Money Order**

Credit Card Number	
Expiration Date	
Signature	

Please Mail to: Book Jungle
PO Box 2226
Champaign, IL 61825
or Fax to: 630-214-0564

ORDERING INFORMATION

web: *www.bookjungle.com*
email: *sales@bookjungle.com*
fax: *630-214-0564*
mail: *Book Jungle PO Box 2226 Champaign, IL 61825*
or PayPal *to sales@bookjungle.com*

Please contact us for bulk discounts

DIRECT-ORDER TERMS

**20% Discount if You Order
Two or More Books**
Free Domestic Shipping!
Accepted: Master Card, Visa,
Discover, American Express